NO FAULT

NO FAULT

*A Memoir of
Romance and Divorce*

HALEY MLOTEK

VIKING

VIKING

An imprint of Penguin Random House LLC

1745 Broadway, New York, NY 10019

penguinrandomhouse.com

Grateful acknowledgment is made for permission to reprint excerpts
from "Wants" from *Enormous Changes at the Last Minute* by Grace Paley
on pp. 203 and 204. Copyright © 1971, 1974 by Grace Paley. Reprinted
by permission of Farrar, Straus and Giroux. All rights reserved.

Designed by Nerylsa Dijol

LIBRARY OF CONGRESS CATALOGING-IN-PUBLICATION DATA
Names: Mlotek, Haley, author.
Title: No fault : a memoir of romance and divorce / Haley Mlotek.
Description: [New York] : Viking, [2025]
Identifiers: LCCN 2024026120 (print) | LCCN 2024026121 (ebook) |
ISBN 9781984879080 (hardcover) | ISBN 9781984879097 (ebook)
Subjects: LCSH: Divorce. | Marriage.
Classification: LCC HQ814 .M56 2025 (print) | LCC HQ814 (ebook) |
DDC 306.89—dc23/eng/20240726
LC record available at https://lccn.loc.gov/2024026120
LC ebook record available at https://lccn.loc.gov/2024026121

Printed in the United States of America
1st Printing

The authorized representative in the EU for product safety and compliance
is Penguin Random House Ireland, Morrison Chambers, 32 Nassau Street,
Dublin D02 YH68, Ireland, https://eu-contact.penguin.ie.

For all my families

I

I was married on a cold day in December. Thirteen months later my husband moved out. We decided to separate in November after agreeing to spend the holidays with our families. We told just a few friends, thinking maybe this was temporary. But the weeks between were a problem. After over a decade celebrating the anniversary of the spring night he kissed me—a hotel elevator, a high school trip—now there was the date that marked the night he kissed me in his mother's living room, where we exchanged rings and signed papers. We had been together for thirteen years, lived together for five, and now, were we supposed to celebrate the one year we barely managed to stay married? Well—we made dinner reservations. Not knowing what to do or where to look, we talked about what we had done that day, our jobs. I tried to be careful but couldn't help making some reference to our situation, so he would know the strangeness was not lost on me. "What was your favorite part of being married?" I asked, smiling to shield the *was*. He talked about our wedding, our move to a new city, and then he asked me the same question. "Being a family," I said, and cried, but only a little.

We flew home. We saw our families, and we fought. We were cat-sitting for a friend and my husband spent his nights elsewhere. The cats had recently been kittens and were not yet adjusted to their adult sizes. They ran and played as though they might not knock over water glasses or pull out electrical cords. They were cute and they kept me awake all night. In the mornings my husband—*my handsome husband*, I sometimes thought when I saw him, even after we decided to separate, because he was, still, both—would come home and feed them, and they would immediately fall asleep. God, I hated those cats.

On the first day of the New Year we flew back to our apartment. By the third day I was living there alone.

Every generation of North American is now alive at a moment when they have access to what is usually called "no-fault" divorce, the legal dissolution of marriage that does not require a reason beyond choice. Those who have lived long enough to know the difference understand the significance of this freedom; those who will never know the difference have inherited a profound question of what divorce should be, who it is for, and why the institution of marriage maintains its power.

I have looked for guidance everywhere but real life. Through fiction and film, through gossip and conversation, through research about the past and speculation about the future, and most of all through work—always working, always writing. I have always preferred reading to reality. In reading, there's the possibility for more than just what's on the page, or the screen, or coming through the other end of the phone. In turning over what happened, the facts are just details, significance just interpretation. This is evasive, and better still, very effective. I want you to ask if I've read *Anna Karenina*. I do not want you to ask what I would do for love.

There are some incidents that seem to matter most and that becomes the story. Sometimes there's risk or danger, tears or blood. A story about broken plates, the screen in the window, the sound of his voice. But what happened after? That is what I want to know.

When they both decided they had had enough, I want to ask: And then what? Did they go to bed, and if so, did they sleep in the same bed? What was it like the next morning—did they make coffee, or say goodbye before leaving for work? I prefer to see myself as audience, watching as though it didn't happen to me. When remembering, I can see that in my story the worst happened twice, maybe three times. Then it was over.

I would like to observe my feelings more than feel them. This is, I know, the bad kind of romance: believing there's meaning to be found if you could get the details right. Only some details matter, but I hold them all with the same weight. Every marriage requires that a couple agree on at least one part of the story: the ending.

I once watched as a person trying to explain something took her pen to paper. Here was a circle, she said, and this was the way most people experienced their memories: as events linked in one round dance with each other, the lines between the beginning of their consciousness and a space stretching out in front yet to be lived. But then there was the way it happened, and the way it was remembered: as a spiral that started low, grew wide, and lapped around and around, touching occasionally, as we perhaps regressed or lagged or repeated a bad habit or spent time in a stage we thought was over. That's the way I find myself trying to describe these years. Not backward and forward, or up and down, but around and around and around and around.

I, like so many, first inherited my knowledge of divorce from my family. Then came my own divorce. On the last day my husband and I lived together, I gave him my largest suitcase—the one I had used often during the one year we were married, traveling for work away from our home, and almost never in the twelve years of our relationship that preceded it—and watched the beginning of him packing. I left before he finished. It took one more year after that day before I told most of my friends and family and loved ones. In that year my life changed so much I couldn't recognize it as my own, while many more days revealed only what I should have already known. Maybe I was waiting until I could tell the difference. Maybe I was waiting until I felt ready. Mostly I was just waiting.

The story my mother tells is: When I was ten, I told her she should leave my father. "It's OK," I reassured her. "We'll be fine." I have no memory of this, although I've heard it enough I can access an approximation. It does sound like one of the deliberately precocious things I said to keep an adult's attention. I remember my bedroom at the time, with the floral comforter, and the shelf above my bed where I kept a lamp on all night, every night. In my memory I am more preoccupied with the dark than I am with divorce. Across the hall was my younger sister Erin, in a room I remember being almost the mirror reflection of mine—the same arrangement of furniture, only oriented toward a window that faced the back rather than the front yard—and down the hall, in the tiny space attached by French doors to my parents' room, was the room they had turned into my baby sister Jackie's nursery.

There are many moments from my childhood I don't remember. I have a better recollection of the homes we lived in: the moves and mortgages that took us to new neighborhoods every few years. The smell that evokes home is, for me, fresh paint. With each bedroom I would try to re-create the same collages on new walls—photos from Caboodles or Candie's ads, images of Sarah Michelle Gellar and Aaliyah—torn from stolen issues of *Teen People* and *CosmoGirl*, the elastic pull of bright blue Sticky Tack close to ripping the thin pages with their coated gloss. I know I always kept my bedroom lamp on, I have always been afraid of the dark, and I always wanted my parents to get a divorce. The other details—I mean, what does it matter? I was, this story proves, a child of divorce long before the day my father knocked on my bedroom door, nine years later, to say he was leaving.

In those years my father was an insomniac. Nobody seemed to sleep in our house, and if they did, they didn't sleep well. I would spend my nights looking up the real story of Anastasia and the Romanovs, or scrolling through the Delia's catalog, or having cybersex in chat rooms.

My parents fought often, their volume reaching decibels I felt through my bedroom door and into my rib cage. The fight was always over money—how much we had, which was not enough for what we needed. The light I kept on in my bedroom was always accompanied by the blue light of the television set my father watched late into the night.

Sometimes my father spoke to himself. This was one of his classic traits; we all teased him about it, which he took very good-naturedly. He spoke to himself while he watched television and while he drove, though it wasn't the same as when he spoke out loud. His voice was audible, but it was like you were eavesdropping on the sound between a thought and a whisper. He didn't seem to realize it as it was happening. Sometimes he would slap the steering wheel or the sofa arm for effect when he got too carried away, and I would flinch, and then he would stop. He was, I think, practicing or preparing for some future conversation. My thoughts are also always in the shape of a conversation, or sometimes perhaps a fight; I inherited that or I learned it. When I consider my own consciousness, I can see that I'm always explaining an idea to some audience as practice or preparation. My thoughts increase in volume the more I focus on them. When I sit still to think, I am almost always holding my hand over my mouth, to make sure the thoughts don't start escaping.

My first memory, as far as I know, is of going with my father to get a goldfish for my mother's birthday. I do suspect this is one of those childhood memories that develop because we have seen enough photos and heard enough stories, but I can kind of sense the feeling of that day. I must have been two, because my younger sister wasn't born yet. In the photo I am sitting in the center of our couch, slightly sinking in between the cushions, the plastic bag half-full of water propped between my legs and the swimming goldfish just a blurred orange smudge. In my memory the plastic of the bag is cold, the couch is too soft, and I am too short when I twist my head around to try to see out the window, checking if my mother is coming up the driveway. Another memory of helping him with a gift, later in childhood: in the days leading up to my mother's birthday he calls the house and asks me to surreptitiously check her closet for her clothing sizes. I don't know what he was planning to buy her, but I know I must have been twelve, because I know exactly which bedroom closet I was looking into at our house at the time. I stood there with the cordless phone, the first moment in what would later be my lifelong confusion with understanding women's off-the-rack clothing sizes: they were all of indistinguishable widths and lengths, and I knew they all fit my mother, and yet all of them had different numbers printed on the tag. "Aim low," I advised him, already understanding that vanity is as good as if not better than accuracy for some decisions, and I remember how hard he laughed.

My mother did not divorce my father when I asked. Instead, she stayed married and became a certified divorce mediator, the business of keeping families together even after they decided to live apart. Our basement was her office, and her office was my first job. She decorated with books written by every expert she could find, and taped construction paper with handwritten quotations from some of them—Jack Canfield, the Dalai Lama.

Beside the books she put up photos of my sisters and me, our baby faces taking on her qualities with every passing year, and her clients would often comment on how much we looked like her. We do look alike, but I doubted they could see that in photos. Mostly we share the same affects. Our smiles are identical and our laughs interchangeable, our eyebrows the same kind of expressive.

I answered her phones and filled in templates on custody arrangements, changing the names of children and their summer camps, their holidays, their parents. *Rachel* will spend *two weeks* with her *father* between *June 29, 1998* and *July 13, 1998*. *Adam* will attend *Camp Tamarack* for the month of *August*. I saved the money I made until I had enough to spend on Spice Girls Chupa Chups, Francesca Lia Block novels, and tickets to movies starring Kirsten Dunst.

I think of the marriages in my life as "my marriages"—the ones I can claim—most of which ended in divorce. My parents', my grandparents', my own. My mom's mother was married twice, divorced twice, and she would sometimes refer, casually, to "my husbands." *Well, my husbands,* she would say to start a story. I thought the plural was the most glamorous thing in the world.

Everything I learned about my mother's job gave me an impression of how divorce worked, if not an entirely clear understanding of what divorce was. At dinner, she would give us general summaries of the couples she counseled, of the ways they had hurt each other long before leaving each other. Like most children I knew, I felt born with the knowledge that not every marriage ended in divorce, but all divorced people had been married. To me this meant being able to end a marriage was a fact as obvious as all the other luxuries I was lucky enough to take for granted, like breakfast every morning and being left alone to read for as long as I wanted.

Also like most children I knew, I felt I had been raised with the sense that divorce was an outcome that our parents resisted yet wanted; that it promised something better on the other side of something bad, and if you could get to that other side there might be, if not total happiness, at least some peace.

That *if* was a big one. *If* you could survive the process, which we understood from experience and from television was one that had the potential to wreck lives and tear apart families. Still, the problems on the other side seemed almost dignified in their averageness. Weekend visits, corny stepparents, smaller bedrooms. With the self-assuredness of a kid who experienced their life as a series of outcomes that they had no control over, and unable to imagine childhood as anything other than the present stretching forever, I thought all change seemed like an equal threat and so a fair risk.

I understood that there were acrimonious divorces, and that there were far worse marriages than I ever saw or heard about. My mother's training didn't cover couples who had much more serious issues between them, like abuse or harm, and she was required to refer them to counselors and lawyers who specialized in that area of separation. Instead, she saw the couples who were, for the most part, getting the common and prized no-fault divorce, their disputes the stuff of property or custody or both.

By thirteen, my voice had begun to sound so much like my mother's when I answered the phone that people would talk to me as though I were her. I felt embarrassed when I corrected these adults, as if I were the one who had made the mistake. Sometimes, when it wasn't a work call, I didn't. Once a mom called to see how her daughter was doing on a playdate with who she thought, based on the conversation she launched into so fast I didn't even have time to say *Let me get my mom*, was not my baby sister but my youngest daughter. Instead I just told her yeah, our kids were doing great, they had played outside and were now watching *The Amanda Show*, they had split a bag of microwave popcorn and a few apple slices, and five p.m. was perfect for a pickup but of course her daughter was welcome to stay for dinner, thanks so much, Sharon, speak soon. I liked the practice of being an adult woman. I figured it would involve lots of similar small lies told easily.

I knew there was something strange about my mother's work. Other children's parents went to offices where they, I thought, shuffled papers between file folders, or typed on heavy keyboards, or talked nonsense in impressive boardrooms. They were nurses in hospitals or salespeople in stores. The closest likeness I could find, when I really thought about it, were my friends whose parents were teachers at the schools they attended. Her clients sat on the same couches I sat on with her. She counseled them on their divorces; I talked to her about the divorce I wished she would get. Even as it became ordinary, I never adjusted to the idea that other people knew my mother professionally the way I knew her domestically. Like a situational comedy or a one-act play, all the drama in our world happened on the same stage.

In the years after I told my mother she should leave my father, I began to think of our home as the place where other families fell apart. What happened in our family didn't seem as relevant as the work that paid our bills. My mother worked relentlessly, daily. My entire world was divorce. All the adults I knew were getting divorced, or should have been. The mortgages paid with money my mother charged for a parenting plan, or a counseling session, or a court date. I remember another precocious thing I used to say to my mother, which I said once thinking it would be a good tagline for her business, and then repeated often because it made her laugh so much. "If you really want to get to know someone," I would say, "divorce them." Later, I would learn this was also the caption of a *New Yorker* cartoon.

I have peaceful memories of being taken to a large local discount clothing chain to select back-to-school or High Holiday outfits, passing from rack to rack silently considering my options while listening to my mother's soft voice on her cell phone with a client. At night, as we ate dinner or watched television, we would hear her phone ring and ring and ring. Everyone thought their crisis was an emergency and everyone was, in their own way, right. To not pick up, my mother explained, was to set a boundary. Why, then, did we not just turn off the ringer? I wondered for years after the fact. Because to not hear the ringing would be a betrayal.

In those years my mother insisted we spend every Friday night at my grandmother's house, to light the candles and eat Shabbat dinner together. This frustrated me for practical reasons—one less weekend night to myself or for my one friend in elementary school to invite me over to her house, to spend the night in her huge bedroom that had a window seat, which was, to me, the absolute pinnacle of sophistication. But the dinners themselves I loved. Early in the evening my parents would drive us to the apartment building where my grandmother lived, the underground parking lot with the mechanical gate and the sloping, scary concrete that led to the guest parking spots.

Her building was occupied mostly by other people her age, part of a complex that centered around a beautifully maintained garden and a small pond, and each week we anticipated what was possible per the seasons and my grandmother's moods. She usually made large and elaborate meals with the same basic elements—always a challah, though sometimes my sisters and I would get our favorite, the one with the powdered sugar and raisins; always some kind of vegetable, which my sisters and I always ate, agreeing to ourselves that we never understood the clichés about kids not liking broccoli, that broccoli was kind of good the way our grandmother prepared it. She would almost always roast a large chicken and then make a vegetarian option for my mother.

Some weeks my grandmother would say she had been too busy or too tired to make a whole dinner, and we would get what was in fact our favorite dinner, her spaghetti with meat sauce; this always annoyed her, that we would get *so* excited to have the dinner she considered second rate, but in a funny way. If it was winter the dinner would have a soup and we would watch *Jeopardy!* after we loaded the dishwasher, which was where I developed my obsession with properly loading a dishwasher. In the summer the dinner would have corn and the dessert would have blueberries, and after we had loaded the dishwasher we could go to the pond and watch the fish.

As a child I was very concerned that our dinner table conversations were not representative of the entire world. How come we never talk about politics, I complained. How come no one had ever told me what was happening in Sarajevo, I asked, because I had seen a headline on a newspaper walking home from school. My dad bought me a book. Later all our dinner table conversations would be fights about politics, so that we wouldn't fight about our family. Most of them circled around facts and semantics, the split hairs of self-educated opinions. *You don't know what you're talking about,* my father would say to my sisters and me when he was either losing the fight or losing interest. We didn't, but there was no way *he* knew that.

In between dinner and the dishwasher, I would wander around that apartment. After her divorce from my grandfather, my grandmother had gone back to work, a series of jobs that became over time less what she had to do and more what she wanted to do: some secretarial work, and then later, she became an art dealer for painters and sculptors, and sometimes worked as an interior decorator for assisted-living spaces. Her apartment, to me, had the most fascinating objects, composed in a harmony I wanted to figure out. Everything stayed the same, but every time I looked, I would see something different. She had paintings of children in snowsuits in her hallway, round, pastel figures on a snowy landscape outside their school; large abstract art in the dining room; jade carved into the smoothest shapes on her glass coffee table. Her walk-in closet led to her bathroom, where every item was in its exact right place— cashmere sweaters, tortoiseshell purses, sensible square-toed shoes. This, I was certain, was exactly the way a grandmother should be. This, I thought, was the way I should be one day.

I would go through her things and bring objects back to ask her what they were. What is this? How do you wear this? What does this do? And she would just laugh. My grandmother had a great laugh, but mostly she had a great way with laughter. She never tipped her head back or covered her mouth from laughing too hard. Even when it was a big laugh she held eye contact and her smile wide open. When she went too far with a joke and delighted in it, her laugh took on an evil pitch that was a joke in itself. When I went too far with something evil and it delighted her she would lean over to add a real slap on my arm for emphasis. After she explained what part of the object's memory had made her laugh she would then turn it over and explain its function—a fan she had brought back from a hot vacation, a silk scarf painted by hand, a measuring tape that looked like a shell made of gold.

W hen I was ten, we were between places to live, and moved in with my grandmother. (The first writing I ever published was right around this time, for a contest offered in a local newspaper—something for Mother's Day. *Why My Mother Is the Best.* I won. My grandmother kept the clipping on her fridge for the rest of her life, right beside a photo of me at a family wedding sitting with my arms folded and my eyes staring off behind my big pink glasses, disappointed because I had been told the bride wasn't going to throw the bouquet. I think I had learned about that from watching *Addams Family Values*.) My parents took the master bedroom, my grandmother on a temporary bed in a makeshift space off the living room. I slept with my sister in the spare bedroom, my sister in the twin bed and me on the mattress on the floor—an endless slumber party, I thought. I loved that time in its own way, the change of interior like a change of scenery. One evening my aunt came over for dinner and we spent most of the night as we often did, by the kitchen sink, delaying cleaning up to keep talking. "Be honest," my aunt said, as the conversation became more and more between my grandmother and me. "Haley's your favorite, isn't she?" Everyone laughed; my grandmother gave her a look, the one that meant it was time for my aunt to knock it off. "I don't play favorites," my grandmother said, and everyone laughed again. The joke was that my aunt would have to ask.

When we did settle on a place to live, my mother maintained an ongoing interest in home security: she saw our home as a refuge and protected it like a fortress. We always had an alarm system, which we would beep off and beep on every time we came or went. At one point she had a man with a business card that titled him a "security consultant" come to the house and discuss options for her office; he suggested, she told me later, either a security camera or a panic button. Which did I think was better? Neither, I told her, but obviously the panic button made more sense, if she was really concerned. What would we do with security camera footage? *Watch her get attacked?* I don't remember being angry when I said that, but I must have been; it seems like an angry thing to say.

I wasn't ever afraid of so many people coming in and out of our basement, though those were some of my most anxious years. By the time I was sixteen I was spending entire nights with the cordless phone under my pillow, listening for sounds of a burglar or similar, poised to save my entire family in case the alarm system failed. I couldn't sleep with my back to the door, thinking that would impede my reflexes if someone burst in. Mostly I stayed up all night throughout my adolescence, reading Wikipedia entries on conspiracy theories, or Literotica stories, waiting for the sun to come up so I could sleep. I have always slept better with a light on.

During my mother's office hours I could sometimes hear muffled conversations—the feelings, not the words. There were always boxes of Kleenex in our basement, behind the arm of every couch and on every table. If I turned my head and looked out the window at the right time I could see the formerly married couple speaking beside their parked cars, their heads low and their tones high. Once, a woman became so angry at her ex-husband that my mother removed the pencils on the table between them. "I just thought," she explained later, "maybe that could be a weapon."

Most couples who go to mediators are not so dramatic. Mediation is an alternative to other forms of judgment, like litigation or arbitration, meant to relieve overcrowded family law courts. It is supposed to be the gentler divorce, collaborative and calm. In the absence of freshly sharpened pencils, couples split their homes, their kids, and their lives fairly and amicably. Today, if both parties agree on what they want, then a binding divorce is papers signed and rings removed.

Legally, this is a progressive solution, made possible by a few hard-won presumptions: that with so many divorces, courts should be reserved for the couples who really need them, and that if divorce is both ruinous and inevitable, then it must be made clean.

Anecdotally, and sometimes statistically, divorce appears as common as marriage itself. A frequently cited statistic is that 50 percent of marriages end in divorce. It's not entirely clear if this is true or just feels true. There are some issues with the numbers, which may, for one, originate from projections that failed to prove true; for another, American federal funding to collect divorce data was reduced in 1996, so some divorce certificates may be going uncounted in courthouses. Self-reporting is a flawed collection method, and gaps in accuracy lead researchers to the statistical practice called "imputation," also known as "guessing."

The Census Bureau has pointed out that lots of people who report that they are divorced (for example, me) do not actually file, in court, for divorce within the same year (also me). This skewed data leads to a flawed perspective, in which divorce is more present than ever even as it recedes into the horizon. Knowing the limitations of statistics—funnily enough, not an exact science—is the closest to truth statistics can get.

But learning statistics has had the effect of confirming them. I find numbers in conversations. One day I read that many divorced people end up committed to remarrying within three years, and I thought, there's no way that's right. That night I went for drinks with a friend who told me her ex-husband had just gotten engaged, within three years almost to the day of their divorce. "I guess he thinks marriage works for him," she said, catching the tiny umbrella before the wind knocked it out of her drink.

Numbers are such an unlikely form of solace, and yet they serve that function all the time. They promise an invisible shared network representing actual people who are, no doubt, wildly different and probably not even people you would want to spend any time with, but the fact of their existence is enough to soothe us in solidarity. They are our comrades, aren't they? And even if we wouldn't want to be invited to their house for dinner or share their taste in magazine subscriptions, we can have a feeling of kinship. The statistics about divorce take on the quality of a fable that warms our own understanding of the world, taken to our hearts so that we might feel less alone.

At the same time, numbers are such an unlikely form of punishment. Random and arbitrary, they are nothing more than a counted total or a precise quantification, and yet they represent a staggering crowd. No doubt we have been to a concert or a baseball game with huge numbers of people and managed well enough, but now in contemplating, those sums feel almost bottomless: every number added is a whole person with a whole life. The statistics of divorce are more like a zombie movie that terrifies with its promise of conformity, of inevitability, overwhelming our minds with the helpless knowledge of the force that's coming for us.

M y parents were born in what is sometimes called the "long decade," or more commonly the baby boom, which begins and ends on either side of the 1950s. In North America, this period began in 1947 and lasted until the 1960s. People married early, and husbands were the sole or main providers across many different demographics in addition to the white middle class. In 1914 Henry Ford began paying his workers five dollars a day, double what he had been paying previously; this was an attempt to decrease turnover and inhibit union-organizing drives, and was contingent on good behavior. Employees could lose it for infractions such as excessive drinking, gambling, or a wife with her own income. He called this salary with all its strings the "family wage." Salaries kept rising following World War II, with more families achieving a better standard of living on a single income; until 1973, wages for white male workers stayed steady with productivity growth. By 1950, only 16 percent of young children in the United States had a mother working outside the home, a figure that had never been so low and would never be that low again. With 95 percent of adults in North America and Western Europe getting married in the 1950s, this decade was also the closest to universal that marriage would ever be. People married younger— the census of 1960 included people aged fourteen to eighteen who married, and with them the statistic is about 67 percent of all adults—and lifespans were longer and becoming exponentially so compared to previous generations, and divorce rates either fell or held steady. A woman born in 1850 could expect to be married for about twenty-nine years before her death. A woman born in 1950 might be a wife for forty-five years.

Our understanding of marriage was altered, if not warped, by the brief benefits of the long decade. The institution had been primarily linked to land and other forms of property for thousands of years, arranged by parents or trusted members of the community for financial or social gain. The family was an economic unit that organized households the way we expect governments to classify citizens today—in it, people knew what they owned and what they would inherit, what their labor was worth and where it was needed.

his is not to say that sex and love didn't happen in marriage. It is to say that sex and love were not the point of marriage. There has only been about two hundred years of what Stephanie Coontz, the author of *Marriage, a History: How Love Conquered Marriage*, calls the "male protector love-based marital model," which was built off a tenuous alliance between existing political beliefs and legal practices drastically different from new Victorian romantic ideals. Opponents of the Victorian philosophy warned that if love were the main reason for getting married, everyone would get divorced. They were right. Divorce became, like marriage, a mostly romantic endeavor—the implication being that *this* relationship didn't work, but the next one might.

There is hardly a beginning to the story of Western divorce. Instead, there are many places to start, which is appropriate for a topic made of endings. One of them remains with an American idea of freedom that refuses to entirely shake tradition. In the United States, divorce has both been the cause of moral panic and taken to be a moral right ever since the colonial era. It is as enshrined in secular American law as freedom from tyranny, and as controlled as a drug. Once Americans agreed they would not be governed by an empire, they applied the same belief to matrimony, suggesting a link between monarchy and marriage that is neither flattering nor romantic. In her book *Public Vows: A History of Marriage and the Nation*, historian Nancy F. Cott describes marriage at the advent of the United States as occupying "the place where political theory overlapped with common sense," a system of shaping the institution that went through three levels of public authority. First, family, friends, neighbors, and other members of a community whose opinions carry significant weight; second, the local laws determining the terms of their marriage or separation; and third, the federal laws or policies that unite their marriage with the concept and practice of American marriage itself.

The founders of the United States were greatly inspired by Baron de Montesquieu and his work *The Spirit of the Laws*, and they relied on it when they were developing a concept of marriage to intentionally mirror the government itself. This thinking made monogamy rooted in Christianity the ideal of a democratic country: being a citizen and being a spouse relied on the voluntary consent between the people themselves. Of course, the law at the time turned a married couple into one person who could consent to exercising their rights in America: the husband. The founding laws used the French term *couverture*, referring to the wife as the "feme covert," and it denied her any sort of right to legal personhood without her husband's consent.

During the time of the American Revolution, leaders believed that the character and conduct of citizens would matter much more in a democracy than under a monarchy. They used marriage as a metaphor for the formation of the United States. "In a republic, the people were sovereign, and the motivating principle was political virtue," explains Cott. "The government would depend on the people's virtue for its success."

Meanwhile, marriage—and with it, the possibility of divorce—was deliberately twisted into ideological views of slavery in the nineteenth century. The idea that they were both, as Cott explains the sentiment of the time, "a relationship of unequals benefiting both parties" was an analogy that made slavery and marriage into a form of "domestic relations." This created, for abolitionists who would join the women's rights movement, a polemical reverberation: "If the two domestic relations were parallel, a person who found slavery repugnant might well criticize the power of the husband over the wife in marriage. . . . They contended that both institutions, slavery and marriage, harbored inequalities inconsistent with American principles of liberty and equality."

Slavery as metaphor for any part of American customs, particularly when used to describe an era defined by literal slavery, was a terrible choice; especially apparent in the case of a feminist movement that frequently prized whiteness at the expense of actual equality. Even knowing that the intention was not to create more division but to simply connect an existing political certainty (that is, that slavery must be abolished and Black Americans must be given equal rights under the law) to another similar idea (that women, too, must be given equal rights under the law) can't explain away the fraught dynamics around the speeches and testimonials and op-eds white women were offering at this time.

John Locke's idea about individual freedom as the state of being the "proprietor of his own person" was an important reference. "The southern slave lacked this essential right to own his person and labor," writes Cott, "and in the newly opened eyes of women's rights activists, so did the wife under coverture." Elizabeth Cady Stanton and her friends from a Quaker community led the July

1848 meeting in Seneca Falls that would inspire hundreds to attend similar future conferences. Cott states that their organizing for the vote has been emphasized retroactively—at the time, participants were more likely to talk about their dissatisfaction with the state of marriage. Stanton wrote to Susan B. Anthony in 1853 to tell her she noticed that the problems with marriage resonated with her audience way more than the question of the vote. "How the women flock to me with their sorrows," she remarked. "I feel as never before that this whole question of women's rights turns on the pivot of the marriage relation."

Some of the same reformers advocating for marriage equality also believed divorce was so radical it would scare away otherwise friendly supporters. Abolitionist and suffragist Lucy Stone apparently believed divorce was more like abortion and infanticide, subjects so taboo that they would repel followers. At Seneca Falls in 1848, the consensus called for women to be granted the vote and to receive full equality with men, but there was no such consensus reached on the question of divorce. Cott writes that "thus the abolitionist Antoinette Brown objected in 1853, 'The wife owes service and labor to her husband as much and as absolutely as the slave does to his master.'" Her friend Stone likewise protested: "Marriage is to woman a state of slavery. It takes from her the right to her own property, and makes her submissive in all things to her husband." Stone kept her own name after her 1855 marriage to Henry Blackwell, symbolizing the couple's intent to repudiate these and other attributes of conventional marriage. Ernestine Rose, a coworker of Elizabeth Cady Stanton's in New York state, urged, "Let us first obtain *ourselves*. . . . Give us ourselves and all that belongs to us will follow."

The analogy was legitimized by constant use, including by Abraham Lincoln in a speech to Congress in 1862: "A husband and wife may be divorced and go out of the presence and beyond the reach of each other," he said, "but the different parts of our country cannot do this." This came at a moment of intense scrutiny and paranoia about the sanctity and integrity of marriage. Many movements were considered a threat to the fragile social order of American democracy and grouped in with women's rights, from so-called free lovers, who sought to abolish marriage, to the economically self-sufficient communities that referred to their breakdown of labor and resources as "Socialist," to the relative explosion of Mormon polygamous marriages. As civil rights entangled marriage and voting with a shared civic duty, racists responded accordingly. Cott tells a story about a member of the Ku Klux Klan who was questioned by congressional investigators—he told them he needed to keep non-white people "from marrying, and to keep them from voting," as though the two were one and the same.

Enslaved people had had no right to consent to or make their own contracts. Once they were free, they could decide to enter into employment or marriage, again linking the contract of work and matrimony as evidence of being a free citizen. The Bureau of Refugees, Freedmen, and Abandoned Lands was set up as the first federal government agency designed to take responsibility for its citizens. Often called the Freedmen's Bureau, it mainly served to turn former slaves into employees, but quickly took on the position of pushing legal marriage to either "create or reconstitute male-headed nuclear families." Many of these families were commitments that had been made and lived for a long time, but the government wanted them to be official. People were, reports Cott, eager to legitimize their families, so much so that bureaus sometimes offered mass weddings to serve as many couples as possible. It was considered an affirmation of their humanity, their rights, and for the bureau agents, a political success. "Slavery is the ghost in the machine of kinship," writes Christina Sharpe in her book *Ordinary Notes*, quoting Saidiya Hartman by way of Judith Butler—a haunting made real through the choice of which ties to bind.

While every state was allowed to decide their own terms of marriage and divorce, they also tended to respect each other's laws—something that became a much more pressing issue when the cross-country railroad was completed, and people could somewhat easily end their marriages by traveling to another state with more lenient laws. Some, like Utah and then perhaps most famously Nevada, began welcoming temporary residents to take advantage of their approach to divorce: no marital legislation was federal, a complicated and unnecessarily confusing situation that many, many couples took advantage of. The patterns throughout the country were thought to determine national character, and marital status itself was a huge determinant of a person's civic status. The idea that a state like Utah, which let judges grant divorces based on their own discretion (the divorcé didn't even have to live there yet, as long as they expressed the intention to do so), actually kept *preprinted divorce forms* ready to go for any name to be slotted into the blank line was a new horror that threatened to stow away on the train ride back to wherever these divorcés had come from. When the idea of federal marriage laws was considered, the US Congress decided instead to survey their citizens' actual family structures. "At the time a new word," Cott writes, "'statistics' meant information arrayed for government uses." The results showed that there were real differences between different places; divorce was becoming more common, yes, but the rate varied depending on the region.

Meanwhile, Canadians were watching all of this with much fear and trepidation, making ethical judgments about how quick their closest neighbors were to end their marriages (conveniently forgetting that divorce was only available in three provinces, and otherwise was sparingly accessible through a special act of Parliament). Clearly, writes historian Dr. Roderick Phillips in *Untying the Knot*, this was "evidence of moral inferiority." On the other hand, there was a steady stream of Ontario residents temporarily moving to Upstate New York to get their own divorces by the end of the nineteenth century. And the economic benefits of being a place where divorce was possible often outweighed ethical concerns: in the 1890s, when clergymen in Sioux Falls opposed South Dakota as a divorce haven, they came up against the hoteliers and other business owners unwilling to give up the profits of divorce tourism.

European politicians, too, worried about the relative ease with which unhappily married people could leave their spouses by leaving their countries: in 1902, there was an international convention in The Hague, attended by a handful of the most prominent nations of continental Europe, with the aim of preventing "any country's becoming a divorce haven for the citizens of others," allowing only laws observed in both countries to be similarly respected. A German citizen, for example, could get divorced in France if the cause was adultery, because both German and French law at the time allowed for divorce for that reason. At the same time, why would a citizen choose divorce tourism if not for something unavailable in their own backyard?

Instead of a federal approach to marriage and divorce, a local one emerged organically. Neighbors, in this time when American people were spread out across a huge body of land and the state had little-to-no way of surveilling them, could do a lot to control what was considered good and bad behavior. The gap between laws and real life always allowed for exceptions, bolstered by liberal ideologies that prized the individual's right to self-determine without intervention, exemplified by John Stuart Mill and Harriet Taylor (later Harriet Taylor Mill), who wrote sometime around 1832 that "marital status should be regulated not by law but by the individuals themselves." Couples were creating more of their own flexible arrangements than religious or government leaders would like to admit. Self-divorce, premarital sex, and bigamy were parts of many white and Christian-American relationships, despite the laws against them. There wasn't much order in enforcement. Local communities especially tolerated things like self-divorce and remarriage if the couple seemed better off for it. In 1828 Andrew Jackson's political opponents tried to accuse him of committing adultery when it was discovered that he had "self-married" Rachel Donelson Robards in 1791, a somewhat regular practice at the time similar to what is now called common-law marriage. The act of "self-marriage" wasn't an issue so much as the reason why: Rachel was still married to another man. Historians have different opinions on whether their communities accepted that she left for good reason, since her first husband was known to be abusive, but reportedly people accepted that she had to do what she needed to do, even if that couldn't yet be done legally.

In the nineteenth century, divorce statutes often only allowed the supposedly innocent spouse to remarry (although that probably didn't stop anyone from getting remarried). Still, that's a powerful legacy to carry into the current practice of divorce law. In our present, which seemingly allows both spouses to walk away absent of fault or blame, the question of innocence has a long, low echo. When spiritual and political leaders throughout history have warned about marriage becoming a purely civic or secular partnership, they were warning about a loss of sanctity—that making the choice a legislative one rather than a sacred one will diminish the institution. As Phillips writes, the liberalization of divorce law was never intended to provide freedoms to those denied them; it was to give more power to those who had more than their share. Could fault, in these circumstances, become a way to maintain at least one form of sacred emotion—in this case, shame?

In 1998, my father came downstairs to use the family computer and found me reading the *Starr Report* with the same dedication I had brought to my library copy of *Anna Karenina* the summer before: full attention and zero comprehension. He laughed, and left me alone with it.

My mother and grandmother would frequently talk about the royal divorce when that was happening, and I had read all of my grandmother's unauthorized biographies of Princess Diana. Now Friday night dinner talk would almost always lead to questions of perjury, American political power, and guarded, laughing euphemisms for blow jobs, while I listened intently and drank the soda pop I was only allowed one day of the week.

In comparison to Andrew Jackson, then-President Bill Clinton did OK when his own marital reckoning came for his political career. He was the first sitting American president to be made to confess his infidelities, and the second to be impeached. He survived politically in no small part because enough people believed that what had happened between him and Monica Lewinsky was ultimately between him and Hillary Clinton. Other presidents had kept their affairs to rumors and gossip. This was on the record, and though no one who lived through that era could say anyone came out of it without consequence, the Clintons' power has only deepened in the years since. Thirty years before this scandal, Nelson Rockefeller couldn't win the Republican presidential nomination because he was divorced. It would be another twenty years before the misogyny and stigma against Lewinsky herself had a similar reckoning.

In that one brief part of the 1990s, Cott describes, Clinton stood without toppling because of "the way people understood marriage at the end of the twentieth century . . . The debacle of impeachment forced explicit public cognizance of marital conduct as private and of marital fidelity as too common a failing to prompt civic excommunication." This came after the French demographer Louis Roussel, writing from the remove of the late eighties, identified 1965 as a year when, across North America, Europe, Japan, Australia, and the Soviet Union, the world was undergoing practically cataclysmic shifts in demographic behavior: fewer unions made official and fewer babies born overall, right beside more divorces filed and more babies born to not-married parents. This was what he called a "canalization" of previously condemned behavior, a way of living so at odds with social standards that the social standards were forced to consider themselves changed.

The Victorian era laid the groundwork for many of the social standards we still recognize, ones that were messy and surprisingly enduring. Their popular sayings included truisms like "Better single than miserably married," and "The insistence that marriage must be based on true love also implied that it was immoral to marry for any other reason." This is a fascinating approach to thinking about commitment: better to be alone with yourself than alone with your husband.

During the Enlightenment, too, advocates for divorce turned over the family unit looking for flaws: marriage, family, and other areas of domesticity looked different under this new light. Debates often turned on the idea that staying married for an entire lifetime was inherently wrong, unnatural. The medieval Church had taken away something that previous cultures and societies had, in their pre-Christianity wisdom, openly permitted. Even more to the point, the availability of divorce didn't seem to encourage separation so much as formalize it. One of the very first legal divorces in Rouen, France, was granted in December 1792 to Marie Piedeleu. She was sixty-six and wanted to divorce her husband, who had abandoned her thirty years earlier; sixteen days later, Piedeleu married a man who listed his current address as hers. The reason for why she was divorcing now is unknown, besides the obvious: because she could.

The reason for why she married the second man is similarly obvious: because they clearly already lived together, and now they could do so as spouses. The only substantial change to the facts of her daily life was what the government knew about it.

The fear that Victorian sensibility would unravel marriage is itself a tradition. In *Marriage, a History,* Coontz writes that the ancient Greeks used to complain about the declining moral standards of their wives, while the Romans pointed to their high divorce rate as evidence that they had left behind a previous time of happy, whole families. Historians have noted that medieval men and women might have used annulments as substitutes for divorce, and early records from the Catholic Church show that they sometimes used the words *divorce* and *divortium* interchangeably with *annulment* and *separation.* The sociologist Amy Kaler was once collecting interviews with people in a part of Southern Africa where divorce was a common practice, and she was told again and again that divorce, as well as marital unhappiness, was new to this generation. When she went back to read oral histories from their parents and grandparents, she found that they had all said the same. "The invention of a past filled with good marriages," Kaler concluded, "is one way people express discontent about other aspects of contemporary life." Critics, pundits, and religious leaders were crying crisis in the 1790s, 1890s, 1920s—when stability seemed to come in the 1950s they welcomed the calm, though this would turn out to be, in Coontz's phrasing, simply the eye of the hurricane.

Marriages during the Great Depression provide what is perhaps the best example of the limitations of reading statistics as a story: the divorce rate fell dramatically, and some interpreted this as a rebound from the hedonism of the 1920s. Writing in a newspaper editorial, one person claimed, "Many a family that has lost its car has found its soul." Meanwhile, by 1940 more than 1.5 million women were living apart from their husbands, which could have been a way of divorcing themselves without incurring the costs of a divorce in court. There was also an incalculable number of spouses who could not afford to move away from one another.

When Francisco Franco took power in the late 1930s, his fascist government had a strong alliance with the Roman Catholic Church. Divorce in Spain was then heavily restricted—if technically legal— and they would have abolished it entirely if not for what Phillips describes as "matrimonial anarchy." Instead, in March 1938, civil marriages were suppressed and divorces were suspended, even divorces already finalized, briefly suggesting that any remarriage would also be void. Pablo Picasso swore that he would never allow *Guernica* to return to Spain until the country was liberated, and up to 1981 his daughter Paloma upheld this wish, saying that the divorce laws proved the country was not free.

The Nazi government quickly and determinedly used the concept of family to further their agenda, with acts such as the Nuremberg Laws in 1935, which included laws against marriages or any form of relationship between Jews and Aryans. Even earlier than that, in 1933, Hitler's government introduced a series of loans intended to economically seduce young Germans into marriage. They were given vouchers for furniture and home goods, and the accumulated debt was partially forgiven with each child the couple subsequently had.

There was a huge incentive to have lots of children, then, and as soon as possible, leading to exactly what the Nazis wanted: a statistically astounding rise in the birth rate and the Aryan German population, all kept safe within the domestic unit. (The marriages were only one part of this plan; the Nazis also shut down centers distributing birth control, banned the promotion of contraceptives, and severely restricted access to abortion.) Oddly enough, their fascist logic approved of no-fault divorce. For purely practical reasons supporting their demographic mission, Nazi law acknowledged that there was no point in forcing two unhappy people to stay together if their happiness could mean remarriage and more babies. They also allowed divorce in the case of, for example, a man who complained that his wife kept shopping at Jewish-owned stores, and another for a woman who said her husband kept "incessantly sneering at her being a member of the Union of National Socialist Women." This woman also accused him of being upset when their son gave a Nazi salute.

Paul Popenoe was the founder of America's first marriage-counseling clinics in the early 1930s, and became famous after appearing on multiple radio and television shows. He is perhaps best known for cofounding the *Ladies' Home Journal* column Can This Marriage Be Saved? and had previously been known as a horticulturalist, whose first book was about date palms, as well as an unabashed eugenicist. The first advice column aimed at wives of this era was called The Companion Marriage Clinic and debuted in *Woman's Home Companion* in the mid-1940s. Making Marriage Work followed in the December 1947 issue of *Ladies' Home Journal*, and while Can This Marriage Be Saved? was initially intended to be a seven-part series beginning in January 1953, it ran in the magazine until 2014, when the print issue was reduced to quarterly and the digital publication was split up among other magazines owned by Meredith, their parent company. Editors would routinely reject questions that came from couples who seemed uneducated, and in one case the *Journal* chose not to work with a marriage counselor because he submitted a question from a couple the editors said were "too Jewish."

In her book *Making Marriage Work: A History of Marriage and Divorce in the Twentieth-Century United States*, Kristin Celello argues that "decades of visits with marriage counselors, of reading advice columns in magazines and newspapers, and of watching portrayals of marriage and divorce on film had ingrained the 'marriage as work' formula in the minds and lives of American women and men." It is not just that they have portrayed themselves as marriage experts that is troubling, Celello notes. It is that "judging by their ubiquitous presence in the media of their respective eras, everyday Americans accepted them as such." Besides their questionable claims to expertise, the first marriage-and-family experts had a few other traits in common. They believed marriage was essential to America, and that the state of marriage was the best indicator of American society. They believed that this pillar of American society was, or would be soon, under attack. And they were racists who believed that the only people who could save marriage were white middle-class women.

In 1958 the show *Divorce Hearing* debuted in syndication on television, hosted and created by Popenoe. Each episode featured two couples who had filed for divorce in a real court, and Celello says it capitalized on the two most significant trends of the so-called golden era of marriage: "the public's seemingly unquenchable thirst for televised courtroom dramas and high expectations for married life that were matched by widespread anxieties about the stability of American marriages." Almost a decade earlier, a lawyer in Chicago had founded Divorcees Anonymous, a group therapy collective that paired recent divorcées with women contemplating divorce, in hopes of talking them out of "similar blunders." By 1956 the organization claimed they had saved three thousand couples from divorce. In the 1960s, an Ohio judge named Paul Alexander believed that most people who wanted to end their marriages had psychological issues that prevented them from being happily married. He, along with other, like-minded legal professionals, applied a concept known as "conciliation courts," which would issue diagnoses instead of divorces, examining marriages through supposedly impartial judges who could mandate therapy and reconciliation as they saw fit. It was wildly unsuccessful, particularly in one New Jersey pilot program, which saw a 97.3 percent failure rate.

Celello writes that marriage counseling services had begun to appear in a "seemingly spontaneous manner" in cities like New York and Los Angeles in the early 1930s, but she points out that clinics with similar purposes had been operating in Europe for over a decade, and there is some evidence to suggest that the first such clinics opened in Germany in the 1920s as part of the Weimar government eugenics program. "By the late 1930s, many marriage counseling pioneers had started to distance themselves from their European intellectual roots," Celello deadpans, "probably because they did not want to be associated with the social engineering programs of the Nazi government." Probably, indeed.

The aligned interests between Nazis and marriage counselors made it difficult to tell who was influencing who. Popenoe, before transitioning to marriage advice, had been an advocate for surgical sterilization of the "unfit" in California, and published a book in 1929 called *Sterilization for Human Betterment*, which may have been a direct influence on Nazi sterilization policies, according to the research of Molly Ladd-Taylor, a history professor at York University. By 1940 there were at least twenty-three facilities for marriage counseling in the United States, not counting the counseling at religious and community centers, or schools, or charities.

Coontz writes, citing the historian Eva Moskowitz, that people who subscribed to the long decade's idealized view of marriage *and* the people who dissented from it were learning how crucial complaining could be. The advice columnists exhorting women to stay married were also promoting a "discourse of discontent" by telling them that they should see intimacy and self-fulfillment as the central experience of their marriage; by reading what a marriage could be, subscribers saw what their marriage was not. This kind of marriage-centric publishing has been around pretty much forever. White women who were not welcome in the workplace have always found a way to make a living—sometimes by telling other white women not to enter the workplace. In 1953, Dorothy Carnegie wrote a companion book for her husband Dale's self-help book, titled *How to Help Your Husband Get Ahead*. In 1957, Hannah Lees (the pseudonym of Elizabeth Head Fetter, the wife of a doctor) published *Help Your Husband Stay Alive!*, which reminded women that their husbands' health was in their hands.

Other surveys, like those collated by the Census Bureau, had their own statistics to share. Couples living together but not married multiplied ten times by 1960, and by 1990, the growth rate was more than five times that of any other type of household. In 1999, the General Social Survey, an annual undertaking by the National Opinion Research Center at the University of Chicago, declared cohabitation to be the standard way men and women entered their first heterosexual committed living situation, as well as for first relationships following divorces. Between 1972 and 1998 the number of adults who did not and would not marry rose from 15 to 23 percent. And finally, the favorite statistic of popular media and culture emerged: the divorce rate was high enough to approximate over half the marriage rates, predicting that one of every two marriages would end in divorce.

With so many adults living in North America and Western Europe married by the 1960s, this was a singular era that Coontz describes as providing "the context for just about every piece of most people's lives." Rather than the step someone took to show that they had become an adult, marriage became the jump someone made to enter adulthood headfirst, the "institution that moved you through life stages," and ultimately, "where you expected to be when your life ended." Coontz compares disestablishment of religion to the present state of marriage, pointing out that religion hardly disappeared when the state stopped providing rights to one denomination while disparaging all others; instead, many more churches and religious organizations formed. "Similarly, once the state stopped insisting that everyone needed a government-sanctioned marriage license to enjoy the privileges and duties of parenthood or other long-term commitments," she writes, "other forms of intimate relationships and child-rearing arrangements came out from underground. And just as people's motives for joining a church changed when there was no longer one official religion, so people began deciding whether or not to marry on a new basis."

T*he Feminine Mystique* was published by Betty Friedan in 1963. Reading *Mystique* now is an odd, contradictory experience—the silhouette of its influence on what is known as second-wave feminism is very present. Today, it reads as simplistic in its ultimate goals and immensely flawed in its execution. Much like any historical document, it's clear that you had to be there to get it. But what Friedan did accomplish was a work that encapsulated an era as it changed. This is the thing about books: readers change, but pages don't.

Friedan had been writing for women's magazines for years, and she used their house tone to argue her points, the structure of a feature print magazine story to lay out the ideas that were not necessarily her own but would become synonymous with her name. Coontz has also written a biography of the impact the book had on the first generation to discover it, and it is a generous reading of the aura that still surrounds *The Feminine Mystique*, one that prizes the feeling the book inspired as much as the text itself. Friedan may "evoke the kind of emotional response we now associate with chick flicks or confessional interviews on daytime talk shows," Coontz writes, but she also "took ideas and arguments that until then had been confined mainly to intellectual and political circles and she couched them in the language of the women's magazines she had begun writing for in the 1950s."

Like with many single works that come to stand in for social revolutions, the impact of *Mystique* was often exaggerated, and there was never a singular or unanimous response. Some sociologists at the time were more cautious, like Robert Nisbet, who in 1953 said that marriage contained way more "psychological and symbolic functions" than any family unit could possibly provide; the same year, Mirra Komarovsky spoke out against the potentially destructive impact that the ideal image of an American wife could have on ordinary women. Only three years later, in 1956, *McCall's* published an article called "The Mother Who Ran Away," establishing a new height for their circulation. When *Redbook*'s editors solicited their readers to answer the question of "Why Young Mothers Feel Trapped," they got twenty-four thousand replies.

Yet when *McCall's* published an excerpt of *Mystique* in one issue, 87 percent of all the letters sent to the magazine in response were critical of Friedan's opinions. And the assumed radical nature of the book, too, was largely hyperbolic—at no point does Friedan urge middle-class white women to abandon their homes, husbands, children, or heterosexuality. She does not dare to explore new ways of building families and relationships. The final chapter, Coontz notes, even sounds a lot like what today's conservatives recommend to women: part-time work, continuing education, volunteer roles in the community. Most important, *The Feminine Mystique* never suggests that women could organize for better conditions in the home; never calls for deliberate, substantive changes in domestic or legislative spheres; and despite the communion it inspired in its readers, *Mystique* is, at its core, a self-help book encouraging women to act as individuals to improve their chances at a happy life by becoming a happy wife.

For many years, Friedan told the same story: that she had led a life observing the contradictions between what she wanted and what was possible, and that she began writing *The Feminine Mystique* because of the years she had spent wondering what was wrong with her that she, in her words, didn't "have an orgasm waxing the kitchen floor." (This was Friedan's favorite rhetorical device, it seems, and one she used often. During a television appearance, she once told a host during the commercial break that if she wasn't allowed more time to speak she would start chanting "orgasm" until she got to make her point.)

But before she was a face of and a symbol for one kind of middle-class feminist reckoning, she was employed at the United Electrical Workers union, where she kept very, very busy. Coontz lists Friedan's activities as including editing the community newsletter, assisting with the babysitting co-op, and working as an organizer for a 1952 rent strike. Her early writings championed the experiences of workers, and the first few drafts of *The Feminine Mystique* apparently included shows of solidarity for the ways Black, Jewish, and immigrant workers experienced their own forms of oppression. The published version, which Coontz justifiably refers to as watered down, still has a few offhand references to Friedan's connection to the civil rights and labor movements.

Daniel Horowitz, who has studied Friedan's political affiliations, believes that her feminism is, at its core, part of her left-wing politics. But publishing *Mystique* as a mainstream work in the 1960s was not anything like publishing a workers' newsletter coming out of the 1930s and 1940s. Even if she couldn't have known what a blockbuster her book would become, she did want it to reach as many people as possible, and that meant avoiding being blacklisted, no matter the cost. The Red Scare came for all manner of people, and no one was completely safe. Rebecca L. Davis pointed out in her book *More Perfect Unions* that just a few decades earlier, in the 1920s, when America was considering federal divorce laws, the comparison between that and the "easy divorce" available in Russia made lawmakers consider a simpler process as "equivalent to atheistic communism." In the early 1950s even the avowedly left-wing magazine *The Nation* felt compelled to qualify, when writing about the release of Simone de Beauvoir's *The Second Sex* (to which Friedan owed a tremendous but barely acknowledged debt; Friedan reportedly considered de Beauvoir disappointing), that the book had "certain political leanings." Friedan's own paranoia meant that she refused to credit her secretary, Pat Aleskovsky, for the work she did on Friedan's manuscript because Aleskovsky's husband had been publicly suspected of being a communist; Horowitz's research itself has since been used to suggest that feminism in America was all part of a "communist plot."

In the epilogue of *Mystique's* ten-year anniversary edition, Friedan looks at her present rather than back or forward. "I've moved high into an airy, magic New York tower, with open sky and river and bridges to the future all around," she writes. On the weekends, she would invite her friends who were divorced, unmarried, or otherwise a part of this family of choice, people who believed marriages could be made into something new. And then there is a rare admission: she writes that perhaps it was easier for her to start a women's movement that changed society than it was for her to change her own life. Still, she can claim accomplishments in both. Friedan says she used to be terrified of flying, but after *The Feminine Mystique* was published, she stopped being afraid. "Now I fly on jets across the ocean and on one-engine air taxis in the hills of West Virginia. I guess that, existentially, once you start really living your life, and doing your work, and loving, you are not afraid to die."

Coontz remembers her own mother in *Marriage, a History*, as well as in *A Strange Stirring*, her history of the impact *The Feminine Mystique* had on its readers. Her mother was an activist who worked to free the Scottsboro Boys in the 1930s and worked in the shipyards during the 1940s, but when the 1950s came she dedicated herself to homemaking. In the first few years after World War II ended, when more people had disposable income, spending on food went up 33 percent, clothing by 20 percent, and household goods and appliances by 240 percent. Marriage offered a tangible material benefit (even if purchased on credit) that really could improve if not people's lives then at least their cooking.

Divorce rates did slowly increase during the long decade. One of every three American marriages in the 1950s would end in divorce. Strict laws didn't stop divorces; couples just learned what to say to judges. Marriages ended, and perjury flourished. A study of Chicago divorces in the 1950s noted that it was "remarkable" to see how many "cruel spouses," both men and women, were striking their partners in the face twice, without provocation, leaving visible marks—the minimum requirement for a legal definition of spousal abuse. Even in the years before then-governor of California Ronald Reagan signed no-fault into law on the first day of 1970, divorce was available, if inaccessible. One of the coauthors of that California legislation said, "We are not trying to make divorce easier. We are trying to make it less destructive."

It would be forty years before no-fault divorce law was allowed in every state. The last was New York, which adopted it in 2010. Divorce in some form is now available all over the world, with two exceptions: the Philippines, where activists and organizers are always fighting for their rights to a divorce, and Vatican City.

That long decade came to represent the apex of what had taken almost two hundred years for marriage to be, as some conservatives saw it, perfected. Suddenly marriage seemed to be forever, in more ways than one: lacking the institutional or personal memory to re-call how radical the idea of a love match was, or the crisis of free love in previous decades, marriage appeared as a mirage in a des-ert. Surely this had been the way things had been done for thou-sands of years—eons! Even when the divorce rates went higher than they had been in the 1920s, sociologists studying the family didn't blink; they were quick to rationalize away the existential threat as something that, instead, made the marriages that lasted even more enduring. Sociologists Ernest Burgess and Harvey Locke, authors of influential studies about the family, wrote that a "com-panionship family"—a corollary to love marriage—"*relies* upon di-vorce as a means of rectifying a mistake in mate selection." The italics are mine.

This calm approach made divorce into a kind of "safety valve," in Coontz's words, for marriages—the idea that they could leave would perhaps, in the long run, make couples stick it out. Even more, they expected that as more couples chose marriage counsel-ing, the rate would either level off or go down. Burgess, I feel com-pelled to add, never married.

Outside of interpretation, the numbers gathered did point to, at the very least, couples who wanted to self-report that they were happily married. But were they happy with their marriages, or with living safely ensconced in a rare moment of economic balance? They were young enough to remember the anguish of world wars and record-breaking unemployment, and old enough to work and shop as they saw fit, so a nostalgia for this statistically brief moment was perhaps inevitable—in remembering how good things were, maybe there was always the fear of how quickly tides could turn. Maybe there was even a sense of relief when it all washed away.

story: It's 1959 and the furnace is broken. The woman who lives in the house calls everyone—the neighbors, her friends, the repair numbers listed in the phone book. No one can come over to help her fix it. She becomes more and more certain it will explode. Her husband picks up the phone at his office only to tell her to stop calling. She carries her two children downstairs to the basement and opens a folding chair in front of the furnace, sits in the chair, sets her kids by her feet. Her oldest daughter asks what they're doing. "We're going to die today," she tells her.

That's the end of the story. It's fifty-five years later. "What did you say?" I asked Erin when she told me our grandmother had told her this at a family dinner I missed. They just changed the topic, she told me.

I was married on a cold day in December wearing a pair of heavy black shoes I'd long wanted an excuse to buy. I wore a dress that cost practically nothing, a jacket priced at even less, and the same makeup I always wore on special occasions, just a little more of it. The shoes were leather, pointed, with a solid platform base that I loved the feeling of almost as much as I loved the look. I wore them the next week, when I had to go away for work, and every morning when I traveled to the office I stared straight down at the way they looked as they lifted off the sidewalk. They were special, and they were mine.

Someone always complimented them back then, before they got scuffed and dulled from such constant wear, but maybe that's not what made people stop commenting on them. Maybe they could sense how much I loved wearing them, that they radiated a feeling of wanting to be noticed for what they meant to me. "I like your shoes," a kind person would say. After a while they lost their novelty, and to be honest they weren't very comfortable for long walks, which became the only kind of walking I did. I put them away for a long time and then one day, out of nowhere, remembered to start wearing them again. The mentions were fewer, but they still got noticed, and even after separating and eventually divorcing I still responded the same way. "Thank you," I would say. "They're my wedding shoes."

On that first day of the New Year my husband and I flew back to our apartment. On the second day, I kissed him goodbye and left him to pack his things in our biggest suitcase. I walked over my favorite bridge and then back, thinking as though I was listening—waiting to hear what I really thought, or felt, or knew.

When it got dark I went over to my friend's apartment to be with him and his girlfriend. I had introduced them just a few months earlier. While my marriage was ending, they had fallen in love. This surprised everyone, them most of all. Just a few months earlier my husband and I had moved into a sublet, thinking that once we were settled we would take over the lease. I sent out a tepid invitation to a few friends who lived nearby for a half-hearted house-warming party: *Come over, hang out, maybe I'll order a pizza or something.* Without furniture we sat on the floor and occasionally went to the kitchen to, as the previous tenant had shown me, pop out the window screen and blow cigarette smoke into the alleyway below. In truth I had done nothing beyond that coincidence of putting my two friends on the same email. When she talked I noticed he watched very closely—that was the extent of my matchmaking insight. Nonetheless, I was forever part of their story as a couple, and I take pride where I can find it. At that time we were sentimental enough to say it was meant to be.

Very quickly my friends settled into a delirious domesticity, real love a great motivator for home improvement, and their place seemed like the place I wanted to be as I considered my first winter of living alone. I wanted to be in his apartment as they hung the prints she had convinced him to frame, watch over their shoulders as they clicked through open tabs of couches that might be more comfortable than the one we were sitting on. I liked to talk to them both, but I often stopped sooner than they would have liked, some instinct keeping my words to myself. They asked me questions and I would tell them I didn't want to answer, and they would exchange a look that let me know they were adding it to the list of things to discuss once I left.

I watched them make a home and only sometimes thought of a fight between my husband and me that had seemed inconsequential in the moment and now, in comparison, changed. I would walk back to my own apartment, holding my gloved hands over my ears against the January wind, feeling the blood close to freezing under that thin skin. When I got there I looked around as I thought my husband might have on his way out: the piles of books and the low, long couch my only concession to interior design. I remembered the way he had said, in between other, more serious injuries, *We never even decorated.*

I wanted to fight him at the time. He was implying that I had never decorated, I thought, that I had left multiple boxes unpacked, full of things I must not have needed or at least didn't miss. I wanted to remind him that all the apartments we'd lived in had been similarly plain, that my style could most generously be described as sparse. I didn't. I felt what he meant. I had not made an attempt to make a home for us. I had hoped that just getting married would mean a home would follow. I held on to that fight, not because the absence of decor didn't matter, but because if I could answer now I would say the truth: I thought I had more time.

When the apartment was my own I loved it. The day I signed the lease in my name was a thrill and a terror. The landlord had almost refused to let me after learning my husband and I had separated. "Can you really live there by yourself?" he asked, a question that did not seem tied to my income. I could. I *would*. I probably shouldn't, but that was none of his business.

Some days as I left for the job I had taken to pay my rent I would pause and look around again before I locked my door: *Look at my home, all mine, I should get a plant or something but it's still nice, I live here alone and I like it a lot.* A regular paycheck affords a lot of imagined possibilities.

A month after signing the lease I became convinced I had bed-bugs. *My bedbugs, all mine!*

I called a company called One-Hour Pest Control and they told me they would be there in six hours. I hoped that only the first part of their business name was a lie.

The guy came in a distressingly ostentatious jumpsuit that made me, for the first time then and never again since, genuinely concerned about what the neighbors would think. But he was thorough and kind. When he signed his invoice with the words "no bedbugs found" I was certain that now I had discovered the most beautiful sentence ever written and told him so. He gave me his pen as a parting gift. "Maybe it'll keep giving you luck?" he said, unsure. I kept it in my apartment, and I never got bedbugs.

My first apartment alone, and my first time living in a city I had chosen for myself, having lived and worked in the place I was born all the years before this one. I felt like I was constantly rating or re-assuring. "I love it here," I'd say, but I always seemed to be striking the wrong tone, like I had something to prove or something to lose. I did love it. I just knew, even as I loved it, that there were characteristics of the city I would never be able to adapt to. The only things I really hate in life are crowds and loud noises. I might dis-like the dark, but I don't like bright lights either. Every day in the summer the heat gave me the headache of a sunburn but I barely went outside. While living there I developed a detachment from my appetite, wanting nothing until all of a sudden I would be overcome by an immediate and almost impossible ravenousness of need.

I moved to New York, which is a place lots of people move to. My expectations were more complete than a city can ever be. Instead I adjusted to the learned obliviousness of being one person in a big city. I would visit landmarks or intersections I recognized like I was visiting an amusement park where the expectation of fun had been, blessedly, removed. I do—I do!—love living in a new place, I'd think. Everything is different, anyway. Some things should also be new.

Days after signing the lease, unable to sleep, I remembered smoking by that open window in front of all my friends and realized how dangerous that was: the window was so wide and tall and without the screen there was nothing to protect me, not even an assumption of safety. *She could lose her balance and fall at any moment,* I imagined everyone had been thinking. And then what if—now I was just pretending to be asleep, eyes closed—I really did fall out the window that night, and died, and everything since had been a hallucination? How much would that explain?

Even I, in my insomnia, could not believe this was a thought I was having, so lucid in its stupidity. Months later, right before I was laid off from the job I needed to pay the rent I couldn't afford, I would experience a similar response. I fell asleep so deeply one night and woke up in what felt like pure darkness, panicked with confusion: my first conscious thought wasn't *Where am I?* but *What do I do?*

I could tell you about our last night, but mostly I think about how the night passed no matter what we did to hold still. My marriage ended when those scenes stopped being scenes. The fights were the same as the conversations and the coffee was made no matter what was said the night before.

The fight I think of as being the first—although there were others before it, this was just the one I think of as the beginning of our end—happened when we were far away from home, on a vacation with our friends. Late at night and very drunk, we screamed at each other. Remembering our volume the next morning was its own kind of hangover. As the sun rose our friends in the next room coughed and I heard it through the walls; everyone who hadn't passed out from rum had heard us fight as clearly as I heard that cough. I apologized—I always did—then I spent more time thinking about his words than I thought about what I was sorry for. "But you're my *wife*," my husband had said to me, and that was enough. Only eight weeks into our marriage, my status in his life was as his wife. I took no pleasure or power in that title. I felt what he meant: that what I was to him should be enough. The next morning he apologized, and I knew he meant it—both the apology and the title. He was sorry. I was his wife.

What happened after that? I don't even know how to answer

that question. Which after? Here is where I wish I had a straight line to follow. There are some moments that seem to matter. As a condition of his visa, he had to stop working for a period after we moved, and I was working more than ever. He got a job, and then I lost mine. We were never in our apartment at the same time. I began to tell other people things I used to only tell him, thinking I was relieving our relationship of unnecessary stress. I was just creating more things we didn't know about each other. We fought. I apologized, over and over again, but I did not change. *Why had I married him?* we asked each other, by which we meant, why, besides the reasons we told other people. I didn't know. Could we stay together forever, was the question I asked, again and again, but what I meant was *would* we. I asked questions of everyone, tried to find someone to tell us what to do: Should we get a dog, or go to therapy, or plan a vacation? Should we move back to the place where we rarely fought, where we had stayed together for years and years, the place where we had known something about each other no one else did?

I never knew what question I should ask but I did, eleven months into our marriage, know my answer. My answer was no. The night I told him I wanted it to be over is the night I think of as our last, for reasons that are obvious and also my own. We were vicious. We were liquid. When we were done I put one hand around his neck and let my fingers touch his ear, my forehead on his shoulder and my other hand on my heart, which had slowed so much I was light-headed. I said his name again and again. I can still hear the way I said it that night. I am not ready to hear it another way.

The next morning everything seemed to count. We woke up an hour before his alarm. He was a visitor now. The apartment was my own, so I could stay in bed and he had to leave. It was unseasonably warm. What did it mean? We asked each other how we had slept, out of habit, and the man who had been my husband said he hadn't, really, that the sun coming in my windows was too much too early. "You should get blinds," he said. After he left I poured coffee in the same mug I used every day. I decided I would not get blinds. I liked the light more than sleep. Then I went shopping for jeans. *Jeans?* After deciding to get divorced? I remember feeling sweaty and strange on what should not have been a hot day, thinking how it would look if anyone knew I was in a dressing room the morning after ending my marriage. I didn't buy anything, and I don't remember how I got home.

The year I turned sixteen was the year I met my husband. We stayed together until we were twenty-nine. We never made a conscious decision to commit to each other so young; we just grew and changed with each other naturally enough that sometime—I'll always wonder now when—it began to seem reasonable to assume we would continue to do so forever.

At first our parents and friends seemed to think it was cute, and we agreed. When my husband went to university, his parents—gently at first—tried to suggest he "test the waters," and when he resisted, they got a little more forceful in their recommendations. Once I overheard my mother on the phone with her sister, saying that sure, our relationship was odd in terms of length and our age, but if we were happy who cared? Our friends offered similar levels of perplexed, begrudging support. *Don't you want to fuck other people?* the more direct among them would ask. *Well, I don't know. Sure. Does anyone ever get what they want when they want it?* We did break up a few times—all those people, we thought, must've known something we didn't—but we always returned to each other. We knew something they didn't.

By the time we moved into our first apartment and began working at our first real jobs, our friends had graduated, moved back to the city we went to high school in, gotten jobs and serious partners themselves. Now we were right on schedule. More than that, it became our thing: other couples had dogs, or couples therapists, or stories about vacations. We were each other's home. We were *together forever*.

We didn't plan on getting married. When we announced that we were, for practical reasons, we joked that we intended to be each other's first and third marriages. We'd marry, divorce, remarry, like Elizabeth Taylor and Richard Burton. Our friends and families cried; everyone celebrated. "You've been together for *so long!*" they would say, as a compliment. We knew.

I married the man I loved because I needed to. Our visas required it, and we wanted to leave our home and find a new one. All of the most important moments of our relationship happened when we were traveling. When we were, geographically, away from ourselves. The first kiss that became our real anniversary happened when we were the farthest away I ever got from any home, on a school trip to Europe. There were hesitant attempts preceding it. We were too awkward at first. Teenagers. But then we rode the elevator back to the floor I was staying on so he could walk me to my room, and I still don't know what came over him but he leaned in and pressed me against the wall and kissed me in a way I know I will never be kissed again.

Before we married, and then often afterward, I would ask my husband if he really was going to love me forever, if he really did want to be with me always. He said yes; he was sure, yes. I wanted to know if he felt certain, and if he could feel, in his certainty, forever. What must that be like, to believe in forever? I wondered, and I wondered frequently, and I wondered out loud. I started to think my husband and I were more certain of who we were to each other before we took titles that meant what we felt. We stopped making jokes about Elizabeth Taylor and Richard Burton. He did not wonder about my certainty or my forever, or at least he didn't while we were together. He only asked me the same question, in reply, once. "I don't know," I answered, honestly.

The first year after my marriage ended felt like a shock, and like what I had been preparing for my entire life. I moved hard and fast, too quickly to feel anything deeply. Everything I encountered had the safety of novelty—a newness I could examine closely, with the distance of not understanding what I had done.

On that first morning of my first year of being alone, I woke up too early, and looked around the way I imagined my husband might have. I remember knowing completely that he was the love of my life, which means nothing that can be explained except maybe that I knew the back of his neck as well as the palm of his hands. It means that to this day I can still sometimes convince myself I smell him on pillows he never put his head on, that he watched my sisters grow up and on Friday nights he would watch *Jeopardy!* with my grandmother. I knew his family and loved them, love them still, miss them all the time; we had all the same friends and we knew we were going to hurt them, too, when we hurt each other. He was the person I woke up next to almost every day for what feels like my entire life, and I have slept better every night I've slept without him, but on that morning I knew I would never again have one night of rest now that we had left each other. Maybe it helps to know that I thought no one would be able to make me come like he did and in a way I was right. Or how I remembered that whenever I was on a plane with lots of turbulence I would think, *I hope I survive the crash because I'm definitely going to want to tell him about it.* He was, as of that morning, no longer the only person I would tell my stories to, or the first person I would tell them to. I didn't know it yet but when he finally became a person I told no stories to at all I would think I had nothing left to say.

Mostly it is that I loved him then in a way I am often unable to speak now because all the words sound like a plea or a beg or a whine. I mean I was married and now I'm not, and when I consider either state I worry it seems more like trying to describe a dream I never had. And I know—*I know*—that the reason for this is in the telling. I mean nothing except the story I know how to tell. The words are the only way to explain and I need to say what happened, but when I do I lose the man and the marriage for the first time and all over again. Maybe what I want to tell you is that I was so relieved on that first morning of waking up alone, relieved even as I felt the one regret that remains to this day. I regret spending the last months of my marriage saying *I'm sorry* more than I said *I love you.*

II

There are three kinds of marriage. There is *my* marriage, which is special: distinct, complex, it defies easy categorization. There is *your* marriage, which is evidence: of how, as seen by me, your values have served or failed you. Then there is *marriage*: the category that presumes an ideal exists at all. But every marriage is turned into stories. There are the ones we tell ourselves and the ones we tell our families, the ones we tell while the marriage is intact and the ones we tell after a divorce. The story we keep private and the one we make public are just two examples.

That there are two sides to every story is cliché. That there are two stories to every marriage is almost science. Once known as "discrepant responses" in postwar North America, it was a phenomenon researchers could not figure out. Multiple studies conducted over the late 1940s and throughout the 1950s and '60s all suffered from the same issue: Why was it that when husbands and wives were asked the same questions they didn't give the same answers? Often—not always—the couple agreed on facts, such as how many children they had, or their address. When it came time to ask about less-verifiable elements of the relationship, men and women seemed to be describing different marriages. How often they spoke to each other, to friends, to their children. How often they had sex. How often they shared chores or split household tasks. Who made the decisions? Who had the power? Men reported happiness, while women reported despair. Researchers wondered if it was an issue of methodology. Maybe the couples didn't understand the questions. Jessie Bernard, a retired professor emerita of sociology at Penn State, wondered about a different methodological issue: Did researchers understand the answers?

In 1972, Bernard published *The Future of Marriage*, arguing that the responses were not and had never been discrepancies. Bernard's predecessors had assumed that within a marriage they would find a unified narrative—that the married couple would see themselves as being an *us* against the world outside. Instead, Bernard, a sociologist who studied the way biological sex and social gender influenced a person's encounters with the world, found that there are as many stories as spouses. She offered a simpler way of looking at the issue: Researchers should expect to see "his" marriage and "her" marriage, the perspective changing the account. The *us* versus *them* question they were looking for was inside the house: spouses saw themselves as partners in a dynamic that was *me* versus *you*.

Written before same-sex marriage or no-fault divorce were accessible, the book theorizes that gender is a simplified shorthand for who has leverage over the other. More than just acknowledging that a marriage might feel different to different spouses, Bernard suggested that in a traditional heterosexual marriage, the husband's life improves, while the wife's declines. Bernard writes in the ten-year-anniversary edition of *The Future of Marriage* that she approached it naively, thinking she would only have to put a systematic framework to what she had already reported in her research literature. Instead, with every passing year, month, week, and day she found herself with a new draft, a new idea, describing the "breath-

less pace" of her own feminist consciousness being raised, and social codes revealed in a new light, as nothing more than another
cloud.

Bernard's focus had two tracks: What is the nature of a commitment that turns a relationship into a marriage, and what lifestyles
accompany that commitment once it's been established? The questions seemed urgent, if overdue. Knowing enough to criticize our
norms, Bernard wrote, is proof they have already lost their hold
on us.

There are three ways to control for forecasting a future: predica-
tions based on historical trends, projections based on statistical
curves, and prophecies based on desire. When people asked what
would happen to marriage, they were really asking Bernard about
"the controls on sexual behavior." Will we become so free in our
love (such a 1970s question!) that marriage will cease to exist? Beyond that, will our sexual behavior and romantic love no longer be
restricted to a commitment model of marriage?

The self-appointed experts and advisers preceding Bernard's research considered marriage to be a benign and beneficial institution that must be protected. Most literature was aimed at convincing
women to think of their marriage as a full-time occupation. (Bernard received a copy of *The Feminine Mystique* the same day she sent
off what would become *The Future of Marriage*.) Any problems were
in their heads and were their responsibility to fix. Part of this came
out of that long decade of the 1950s. It is not only that the other
experts and advisers had reason to believe these trends would continue; it is that they *wanted* them to continue. They spoke to and
about the American family as though with the right guidance prospective husbands and wives could be swayed in the right direction,

which became the conservative idea of marriage still with us today: one man, one woman, the kids, the car, a house, a porch, a flag.

Another very 1970s question was: Why should things stay the same? Why should consistency matter more than change? What was tradition compared to something true? An egalitarian marriage could be a harmony, with spouses playing different parts at different times. Bernard believed power should be downgraded in both sexes. At the time of her research, however, the dissonance was extreme. She wrote that there are "few findings more consistent, less equivocal, more convincing than the sometimes spectacular and always impressive superiority on almost every index—demographic, psychological, or social—of married over never-married men." It was so reliable, insurance companies factored it into their clients' life expectancies.

Married women, in the same surveys, showed much more uniformly depressing results. While their husbands were serene, married women reported feelings of anxiety and unhappiness; they were more likely to consider themselves passive and phobic. Bernard called this the "shock theory of marriage": the idea that marriage "introduced such profound discontinuities into the lives of women as to constitute genuine emotional health hazards."

The quick-fading phase of romantic idealization is also known as the "honeymoon period." In research literature this is called "disenchantment." Marriage made women feel less independent, less impulsive, less themselves. Their self-image declined the longer they stayed married. John Cassavetes, the film director who collaborated with his wife, Gena Rowlands, on movies about exactly this, once said he believed all women are "driven crazy by playing a role they can't fulfill." Bernard says, "It is wives who are driven mad, not by men but by the anachronistic way in which marriage is structured today—or, rather, the lifestyle which accompanies marriage today and which demands that all wives be housewives. In truth, being a housewife makes women sick."

One study cited by Bernard showed that 73 percent of husbands tended to overestimate their own power, while 70 percent of wives underestimated theirs. Both spouses were deferring, they explained, to who they thought had "the right" to make a decision—in this case, the man—conforming their marriage to a presumed model. When Bernard concludes the portion of the book detailing this concept, she summarizes with a cutting analysis: "His, not bad, and getting better; hers, not good, and badly in need of change."

In the 1970s, when people started asking questions about their rights and responsibilities to each other and to their homes, this could have looked like an absolute galling abandonment of an entrenched social order. But there were lots of other changes to account for, too. In the Depression era, economic precarity kept people at home; in the late 1970s and early '80s, globalization was creating an increasingly unstable and chaotic experience of work, with human labor devalued to the point of nonexistence. People lost their jobs to exploitative profit margins and technologies they had never been trained in, and fluidity seemed a logical response to an illogical moment. If one could expect to have multiple careers over the course of a lifetime—maybe even in fields that didn't exist yet, or in places they had never even visited—then family structures would have to be similarly adaptable, even unconventional.

To agree on what marriage is requires agreeing on a unified version of history. There are, Bernard writes, as many possibilities for pasts as there are for futures. What was common was not necessarily total; what was average was not always thought to be normal. Does marriage have a single past? No, says Bernard. It has as many pasts as it has futures. "For the past has been as varied as the present, with a meandering course and scores of tributaries, large and small, and many potential futures," she tells us. Later in the book I found a beautiful sentence she had written: "The future does not hit everyone at the same time."

One Sunday morning I went to see Esther Perel speak to a mostly coupled crowd. Perel is, in many ways, an heir to Bernard's work. Readers, listeners, and clients alike gravitate toward her balanced, gentle view that marriage is neither natural nor unknowable.

The field of relationship experts and marriage advice still largely comprises people who use shame or intimidation as a tactic to keep people married. Perel has made a name in contrast to those qualities, championing communication and compromise with calm precision in both her writing and speaking. An in-demand couples therapist with a very expensive practice, she is also the author of the bestselling 2006 book *Mating in Captivity*, which offers both a cultural history of romantic commitment and a counterpoint to some of the more insidious ideas about love and sex disguised as tradition, such as whether monogamy is inherently a moral practice, or simply the most common.

Perel's success is best measured by the metrics of our contemporary prophets—TED Talks with tens of millions of views, and a popular podcast, *Where Should We Begin?*, in which each episode follows anonymized couples and people receiving relationship advice of all kinds through their sessions with Perel. At the talk I attended, I sat alone behind two women discussing their self-help books in progress (one was writing a self-help book, the other was reading a well-known title). The rest of the row was taken up by two husbands and two wives, seemingly on a double date. It seemed like the exact overlap of people who can afford a ticket to see Esther Perel speak but cannot afford an hour of her therapy.

The future of marriage seems unknowable, Perel writes, only if no one learns history. At the talk, she led the audience in small but increasingly revealing group exercises. She asked us to stand if we were in a couple; she told us to stay standing if we wished we were not. "There's never been a time in which a person could say, *I've been monogamous in all my relationships*," Perel gently chastened the crowd, correcting our tendency to view now as eternity. Monogamy once meant that the first person you committed to was the last person you would be with. Serial monogamy is a contradiction of terms. These intimate disclosures made obvious to a crowd should have been embarrassing, but it's hard to feel singular when everyone around you is so obviously the same.

In the question-and-answer portion of the talk, a woman asked for advice on what she considered an infidelity in friendship. After forty years, she and her husband were horrified to learn that their closest couple friends had opened their relationship and were describing themselves as polyamorous. She did not want to support what she considered immoral behavior. Perel gently suggested the woman could ask herself what she considered so abhorrent about polyamory, and to reconsider making such a harsh judgment before ending the friendship. On the way out of the theater I happened to stand behind that woman and her husband, who muttered under his breath, *That's easy for Esther to say; she doesn't have to have dinner with them.*

In the first months when I was separated from my husband I tried to keep a journal, less for my own thoughts than for a straightforward record. Now when I reread it I can't remember what I was saying, or why.

Eventually I grew tired of trying to write down my thoughts. I wrote down other things I heard. Perhaps the journal did something to my memory, because since then I have often thought about one story I know is in there. It goes like this: A woman often speaks to me about a man she says she loves but has never been in love with. He was, she would explain, a great friend during a time of real crisis. She had broken up with her boyfriend after years and years, and this man she loved had taken her side, even though he had been her ex-boyfriend's friend first. He had been through a bad breakup, too. He got it. They would talk a lot about how you can tell a relationship is over when you catch yourself thinking that a person needs to be figured out, when what made you want to get close is the same thing that makes you need distance, and then all your thoughts begin with *Well, what's wrong with him is* . . .

He had a guest room in his apartment and some nights, in the weeks after the breakup, she would stay. The windows in this guest room, she explained to me, were so high, and they let in the most gorgeous light in the mornings. She would wake up early and watch the weather move toward the foot of the bed. She always thought it was weird that her friend hadn't made this room his bedroom. One Saturday morning she woke up and walked down the hall toward his open door, keeping her feet inside one long strip of wood for no reason other than to concentrate on movement instead of decisions, and got into bed with him. Nothing *happened*. They never even touched. He just moved over a little, and they both lay down and went back to sleep without saying anything. When she woke up, she turned her head and saw that his window looked out onto a street of cherry blossoms, so to him the sky was replaced with flowers.

But what's the view like in the winter? I asked, not at all moved by the idea of a man who would choose seasonal blooms over sunrises. She didn't know, she told me. She didn't stay there anymore. They stopped talking once she figured out what was wrong with him.

This was one of the few times I've heard a story about a couple—any kind of couple—and felt sure I knew the truth, if not what really happened.

M arriage experts and marriage counseling are the crux of the belief that marriage is work, and only labor can keep it intact. As such, it follows that a professional field requires professionals. Rebecca L. Davis's history of marriage counseling, *More Perfect Unions*, is an extensive study of the origins of marriage counseling as a movement, which consisted first of formulating and selling it as a legitimate practice. My mother became an expert in divorces and families after the practice of marriage counseling achieved a certain level of prestige, and more than that, a certain level of standardization for training. This was not always the case. The people who were first to assign themselves the role of expert knew more about authority than they did about marriage.

As attitudes toward divorce changed, so did attitudes toward marriage counseling. In the 1950s counselors had considered their clients to be too immature for their marriages; in the 1960s and 1970s, people began to talk a lot about "communication," a slightly more egalitarian distribution of blame between couples. "Conjoint marital therapy" was introduced, allowing therapists to see what happened when spouses spoke to each other, rather than rely on one side's interpretation of events. Practitioners began to wonder if they should be helping people adapt to divorced life rather than pressuring them to stay married. Books such as *Creative Divorce: A*

New Opportunity for Personal Growth and *The Courage to Divorce* were published; the editors of *Ms.* and *Redbook* frequently included stories of women who struggled to end their marriages but were ultimately glad to have done so.

Elsewhere, journalists published stories with titles like "Are We the Last Married Generation?" and "The War on the American Family." In 1987 *Newsweek* published an article titled "How to Stay Married: The Divorce Rate Drops as Couples Try Harder to Stay Together," and around this time, Kristin Celello notes, *commitment* became the catchword most associated with marriage, over *communication*.

More recently, media coverage about the lack of no-fault divorce tended to center around marriages that are by any account long over but stayed legally intact because spouses did not have access to the resources they needed. "Any law that prescribes that people must live together if the marriage is broken is wrong," said Judith Sheindlin at a 2007 conference hosted by the Association of the Bar of the City of New York, called "The Need for No-Fault Divorce," in her trademark rhetoric: firm, sardonic. Sheindlin is more commonly known by her television moniker, Judge Judy.

The field of divorce experts continued to adapt their advice to the times, particularly as psychology and mediation became more common. Dr. Constance Ahrons, who passed away in 2021, was one such advocate for the predecessor of what would later be known as "collaborative divorce." According to her *New York Times* obituary, she lived as a divorced woman and worked with divorced couples long before no-fault was "in vogue." The concept she would become best known for was the title of her 1994 book, *The Good Divorce*, a combination of reflections of her own experiences, legal precedents, psychological studies, and advice for ending marriages and co-parenting children that suggested healthy boundaries rather than saintlike compassion.

The introduction starts with Ahrons's anecdote about her eighty-five-year-old mother proudly telling a friend of hers that her daughter was writing a book. "It's called *Divorce Is Good.*" Ahrons corrected her, thinking she had misheard. No. Up until her mother passed away years later, she would always claim that the book was called *Divorce Is Good.*

This deliberate miscommunication is, in many ways, what a certain class of educators, experts, therapists, and authors struggled with in the years after no-fault divorce was first introduced. Books that help us understand the recent past have an adverse relationship to the future. Every self-help book promises to be the last one a reader will ever need, and yet somehow the obvious contradiction of that feeling does nothing to the feeling itself. Vacillating between horror and romance was the chance to start telling what read like a pragmatic fairy tale: perhaps divorce could be if not good then at least better than the alternative. In the way a marriage could be hard and still good, a divorce could find a way to be both, too. In 1994, when *The Good Divorce* was released, almost half of all the marriages in the United States the prior year were remarriages. People were not done trying, despite the punitive or shameful sensibility that divorce was both inevitable and a failure.

Ahrons began working on *The Good Divorce* in 1976, teaching at the University of Wisconsin and running a private practice as a family therapist. She saw firsthand the "terrifying disorganization" divorce causes; she saw people who had divorces that could be called good or bad, or sometimes both. But the book was written primarily as a "powerful antidote for millions of divorced parents: an antidote to the negativity of society about divorce." Ahrons saw the prevalent stereotypes of vicious, destructive divorces (she refers to this prejudice as "divorcism") as covering up the truth about most families that happen across two households: "an already existing but generally unaccepted cultural phenomenon," she called it, these good divorces might not make headlines, but they could be models of "a quiet social revolution."

Her own divorce was a hard one, in her telling; she notes that she and her husband filed in 1965 without the option of no-fault. Because they were forced to then prove who was at fault, the separation was rooted in fear of social shame and economic punishment, and it went so badly it would eventually lead to an instance of

child-stealing between intensely bitter legal battles. Without the option of simply gesturing to the catchall of "irreconcilable differences," Ahrons had to stand before a judge and tell a story she knew
would meet the standards for "cruel and inhumane" behavior, as it
is called in courts. "My lawyer, the judge, and I all knew I was mag-
nifying petty incidents into major abuses, in order to concoct suffi-
cient evidence," she recalls. It took two years for the divorce to be
finalized, and a subsequent ten years before she could pay off the
accrued legal fees. But like she promises in *The Good Divorce*, it's
never too late to make your divorce into a good one, and over time
she and her ex-husband learned to coexist.

Ahrons describes her research, a longitudinal study of family relationships after divorce, as the first to study "normal" families,
which I took to mean ones in which there is no diagnosed illness,
evidence of acrimony, or known abuse. Much of the research that
existed focused on "families with some psychiatric history, families
with some identified problem or dysfunction." Randomly selected
from the pool of public divorce records in a Wisconsin county,
ninety-eight families provide what Ahrons believes was the true
norm of a geographical area (rather than all divorced families). She
calls this formation a "binuclear family," which remains a unit even
though the members live in two households. Ahrons, along with her
graduate students, ended up interviewing 287 people over a period
of five years, with only two families dropping out of the study alto-
gether.

Much like with Bernard's studies, the details differed when Ahrons
interviewed couples separately. Sometimes they reported different
information on when they had separated, who requested the divorce, how often one spouse saw the children, and how much child

support payments were. Some of this, again like with Bernard's research, was based on gender, while other discrepancies were attributed to personality types, or rooted in the positions they had taken for court cases to win support or custody. If she and her grad students had deleted the names from the interview transcripts, Ahrons said, the differences would have made them unable to match who had once been married to who.

D r. Roderick Phillips began working on an updated version of *Putting Asunder: A History of Divorce in Western Society* in 2022. I called him and asked if he could think of what legal or cultural shifts would be included in the new edition. "Everything has changed," he said. Phillips wrote *Putting Asunder* in 1984 and published it in 1988, when no-fault divorce was not as readily available—Ireland and Italy were two countries in particular that have since seen remarkable legislative shifts. "Generally, the procedures have become a lot simpler . . . and then there are a number of social issues surrounding divorce, such as a greater receptiveness to accepting accounts of abuse (although it falls well short in practice). And then there's the whole issue of custody that's still very much in flux about what the best interest of the child means." Phillips recalls that the stigma around divorce was so great that a divorced person in the 1960s might have trouble getting a bank loan or mortgage, because to be divorced was a sign of instability. Now, by contrast, he points to a "normalization" that naturally occurred as no-fault divorce became an option and people adjusted their expectations of themselves and each other.

Of course, there can be no change to divorce without change to marriage first. Beyond the changes to divorce law, there are fewer marriages overall. People choose cohabitation or common-law relationships, get married much later in life, or marry multiple times over the course of a life. Heterosexuality is no longer a compulsory part of a legal marriage. An assumption that divorce follows infidelity has partially faded, but parts of it still remain. To Phillips, the notion that marriage equals fidelity is still present, and "for all the talk about open marriages, I think they're pretty rare."

There are other stigmas that present differently in contemporary times. When Phillips was writing his first edition, he saw domestic violence as something that was tolerated and that victims were taught to hide as shameful. Physical and mental abuse are both recognized as a legitimate expression of cruelty, and—at least in theory—understood to be neither the victims' fault nor their responsibility.

I wanted to know if Phillips has seen any surprising precedents for the way divorce is treated today, anything that would seem perhaps more contemporary than we expect of our historical traditions. "Yes," he said. "The whole question of romance or attraction in the history of marriage. There are some people who argue that people got married for practical reasons, and it's true in many cases: the people they married were similar in many respects, and when they got together they were able to function as an economic unit. If you went ahead and said, *I really like the look of this person, let's get together because he or she is sexy* . . . I mean, that's fine, but it's not going to help you live. You can't survive on looks or personal charm in those kinds of circumstances. But at the same time, personal attraction or whatever you want to call it *did* play a part. I suspect that's still in play today. We have this sense that it's all about falling in love, but we make decisions before we fall in love; it doesn't happen randomly.

"This is before online dating, I should say," Phillips amended, "that you tended to meet people like yourself at work, at university, at the institutions where you were. You make these decisions as you go that filter people out, and then you end up with somebody who is very like you in many respects."

I told Phillips my favorite joke—that not everyone who gets married will get divorced, but everyone who gets divorced has been married—and he told me one of his own. He was giving a lecture soon after his book had come out, and he was asked why divorce was becoming so common. "I turned around and said, 'The question shouldn't be why is divorce so common, but why was it so rare in the past?' I started the talk by saying that I had studied divorce in ten countries from a period of the Middle Ages to the present, and I'd tried to find out what unites these tens of thousands of divorce cases. I said to the audience, 'I just realized what it was. I'm going to tell you for the first time what unites them all. I have concluded marriage is the main cause of divorce.'"

Because of the punishing rewards that the TikTok algorithm provides, the time I've spent on the app often comes with a lot of divorce content. The sensitivity and responsiveness of that data-driven feedback loop came to know me well enough to hurt my feelings. More than that, the platform knows how to convince me that time spent there is not time wasted. I've watched other people celebrate a divorce or mourn a marriage, listened as the more charismatic kinds of lawyers offered astute or bizarre interpretations of their clients' predicaments.

There is one divorce lawyer who appeared regularly on my feed, a man named Justin Lee whose account is titled BREAKUP LAWYER JUSTIN, styled in all caps just like that. In some of his videos he is disheveled and drinking red wine out of a stemless glass, the better to give his tough-love style of advice the feeling of late-night confidentials; in others he responds directly to some of the popular and toxic unsolicited advice that comes from other accounts. In one, he interrupts a man who is saying "Never marry someone who tells you how much money they make" with "Never marry someone who *doesn't* tell you how much money they make." He uses the popular meme formats to joke about how his motives for getting into divorce law are a mix of altruistic and theatrical: he loves to help people, and he loves drama. In one of his most widely viewed videos, he succinctly describes the reason why divorce law is considered as—if not more so—dangerous as criminal law, using language that seems like a monologue out of a network legal procedural. While criminal law can be understood as bad people on their best behavior, he says with his tie loosened and his sleeves rolled up, divorce law is good people on their worst behavior.

This dichotomy is a good fit for a divorce lawyer, in which the nature of everything he does will come down to one side versus the other. Even with the prevalence of collaborative law and the popular theories about good divorces, the fact remains that all court documents record cases as one spouse versus the other—a break that requires what was one to become unquestionably two.

One popular format for both sincere and satirical videos was the concept of "the stay-at-home girlfriend," vlogs of a day spent by a woman whose full-time job is something like a homemaker but who isn't currently married. Sometimes they are elaborate displays of wealth and involve extensive rituals for grooming and hygiene, from nails and hair to outpatient cosmetic surgeries; sometimes they are ingenious, if obsessive, displays of cleanliness and cooking skills. They are easily parodied since the real thing is already so close to a joke. Lee responded to one that seemed legitimately sincere with a pragmatic legal perspective. "Nothing is ever free in this world," he says. "The price you pay as a stay-at-home girlfriend is your autonomy, your freedom . . . what happens when your boyfriend breaks up with you ten years down the line? You'll be a thirty-five-year-old with no job experience, no career. . . ."

Marriage and divorce laws, for all their gestures at equality, are still ways for states and governments to determine which relationships matter most, a value given to citizens in exchange for the value their commitment supposedly brings to society. Like Bernard's statement about questioning norms being the surest way of knowing that they've lost their power, to consider the imbalance of power in this relationship purely in terms of what laws exist now is to miss all the ways the laws have been and could still be. The law is not really a way of determining how people's lives are, or even how they must be; it follows the change that happens in ordinary lives as a result of extraordinary action.

The courts are also not exactly the best forum to debate right and wrong. They are a contest of last man standing, in which winning is determined as much by who has the time and money required to pursue a lawsuit to the very end as it is by any scale of justice. A woman who has offered her labor in exchange for shelter and security instead of wages is not only at risk of not being able to afford either going forward; she is also at risk of not being able to afford a lawyer who can argue her case, or that it's worth considering a new precedent, or that it is an exception to an existing one. Any spouse who cannot afford a lawyer's retainer does not have much chance of being equally protected by the possibilities of the law.

On the other hand, we are no longer living in a time that offers only white men access to education, property, bank accounts, and marriage licenses. Often these legal warnings have to be taken as they really are, which are sales pitches for a service. No matter how much you love each other now, no matter how collaborative the law gets, these counsels ask, can you *really* get by without a lawyer advocating for your best interest? Other times they are hand-wringing, not unlike the faulty social statistics about the prospects of the unmarried woman, making the world outside marriage seem too dire to be risked, or at least to be risked without the help of a highly paid professional.

Despite what is perhaps our well-earned cynicism about the prospects of marriage, or wry satirizing about the promise of lifelong love, there's still a taboo around talking about either in terms of economics. With any marriage—and now, too, with any of the popular forms of cohabiting or co-parenting—there is the potential for transformative material change to everyone involved in the making of this new family, for better or worse. Getting married is one of the major factors in determining a person's class and wealth, and even the most modest joint incomes will still get a couple further than many single, self-supported households. Rents might become halved, utilities can be split, and you are free to send out requests that someone buy you the really, really expensive salad spinner that you want but could never justify paying for yourself. Single people rarely, if ever, get to demand their friends and family furnish their new homes.

I wonder if the taboo around openly discussing the material facts of marriage, beyond anything offered as a gift, is lifted only when the discussion turns to divorce. In divorce, so often our conversations become strictly business—a numbers game, in which whoever gets the least must be the loser. There's a logic to this. (After all, discussing money now is hardly sacrilegious—how can you defile a relationship that is already dissolved?) There's also maybe a perverse relief. In the stories about prenuptial agreements and statistical eventualities, in the pitch for legal fees and calculations of what the sense of a home is worth, everything that has been lost can be added up to a total owed.

Contemporary marriage has never been pure romance. It remains not just a form of social capital, but a tenet of social insurance. Often it is used as a replacement for all the ways Western countries have failed to take care of their citizens, laid out right in the vows: the answer to the question of who will take care of you in sickness and poverty alike. As Melinda Cooper writes in *Family Values: Between Neoliberalism and the New Social Conservatism*, her 2017 book on the way liberal and right-wing ideologies coalesce around the family unit, the unfinished reforms of the New Deal "left the United States with a fragmented healthcare system, one that reserved privileged workplace benefits to the full-time, unionized worker, most often a white man, and his wife, while reserving an inadequate and expensive public health insurance system for the indigent and disabled."

In March 1970, when a loose collective of about thirty women staged a sit-in in the office of John Mack Carter, the *Ladies' Home Journal*'s editor and publisher, they demanded a "liberated" issue of the publication. The column Can This Marriage Be Saved? was noted as being emblematic of the way the magazine was demeaning to its readers—the answer was almost always yes. The journalist and critic Ellen Willis, a founding member of Redstockings and an integral part of the radical feminist organizing happening at that time, supposedly suggested that they rename the column Can This Marriage.

As a result of the protest, the magazine did publish a "liberated" edition in August 1970. Under their tagline ("The Magazine Women Believe In"), hot pink cover lines promised to solve the dilemma of wearing a midi-length dress, a profile of Joan Kennedy, a story by Bruno Bettelheim with advice on how to say no to a child without guilt. At the bottom, in black text, was: "'Women's Liberation' and You: The Special Feminist Section Everyone's Been Talking About."

Perhaps to show his good-sport mentality, or perhaps to maintain control of what would follow, Carter wrote the introduction himself—not answering the question of what, but why readers would flip through the following eight pages in the issue. "Fifty years ago this month, sometimes using tactics that enraged the nation,

American women won the right to vote," he began solemnly. "But the suffragettes left the job unfinished, and now a contemporary wave of activists has arisen to improve the feminist condition." Crediting their tactics as both "daring and bizarre," he says that they had been following the movement, but that "it wasn't until 200 of these new feminists marched into the *Journal*'s office and stayed for 11 hours that we were literally confronted with the intensity and the reality of this brand of women's rights thinking." (He seemingly cannot help himself from characterizing the discussion as having some merit, "beneath the shrill accusations and radical dialect.")

Now, he warns that his readers may find what follows strange or wonderful or confusing or all three. He also claims that the editing style is more "permissive" than usual, perhaps to distinguish it from what he seems to suggest are the more rigorous standards applied to other pages. Still, he is full of pride for his decisions. "As a magazine that for 87 years has served as an emotional and intellectual forum for American women, we can do no less than devote part of one issue to an explanation of Women's Liberation." Sounding remarkably similar to Betty Friedan's own critique of second-wave feminism, he concluded by saying that this "new movement may have an impact far beyond its extremist eccentricities. It could even triumph over its man-hating bitterness and indeed win humanist gains for all women—and their men."

The introduction written by the collective is called, simply, "Hello to Our Sisters," and includes the full list of demands from their sit-in: a women-led editorial team, reliable and consistent childcare, and a minimum wage of one hundred and twenty-five dollars per week among them. (They won the eight-page supplement and an agreement to a future conversation about daycare.)

"We do not seek to impose a 'line,'" they reassured. "We seek to raise new questions, to analyze the condition of womankind, to search for new answers. Consider this a women's liberation sampler . . . And when you have finished, write to us and tell us what *you* think." Stories included essays on the divisions that concepts of beauty can create between women in the movement, and practical how-to guides on starting one's own consciousness-raising group printed beside a list of existing women's liberation groups and magazines available in densely populated cities such as New York and Los Angeles, as well as slightly smaller places: Buffalo, Cleveland, Kansas, and Vancouver. And when it came time for the spot reserved for Can This Marriage Be Saved?, it was called, instead, Should This Marriage Be Saved? The wife in question was named Barbara, married to a man named Bill; she was a mother of three, and for once the advice was that her marriage could and should not continue. "If Barbara had told her story to a marriage counselor," the collective warned, "you may be sure the answer would have been yes . . . Perhaps Barbara and Bill would have saved their marriage. But they would not have changed its fundamental nature."

Barbara did end up getting a divorce, and the column includes a follow-up report: Since then she'd made friends with many other divorced women, who were drawing up "A Bill of Rights for Divorced Women." Proposals included financial assistance for housekeeping, babysitting, and household expenses; halfway houses to be operational in every major city, so that women would have a safe space to stay in transitional moments; and divorce centers that offered all kinds of guidance, from professional and legal to psychological and social. "If we have marriage counselors," they ask, not entirely rhetorically, "why shouldn't we also have divorce counselors?"

Many organizing efforts of that decade turned over a similar question: Who could help our people learn to be divorced? *Ladies' Home Journal* was targeted because, like so many magazines of that era for that readership, it purported to offer not just advice but answers on all questions of how to be a woman—and, perhaps, a person. Despite the conservative right's attempts to paint the second-wave feminist movement as somehow prejudiced against white women who stayed home to care for their husbands and children, there were many organizing efforts to protect the economic and emotional rights of that exact demographic. In a 2014 paper published in *The Journal of American History*, Lisa Levenstein, the director of Women's, Gender, and Sexuality Studies at the University of North Carolina, Greensboro, characterizes this as an attempt to draw in women of older generations and to convince them that feminism had a place for them.

Meanwhile, the right was successfully organizing a conservative backlash against the gains of feminism and civil rights, with Phyllis Schlafly leading the cause against ratifying the Equal Rights Amendment and Anita Bryant and Jerry Falwell crusading against the rights of queer people. (A former Miss America contestant, Bryant would later, in 1980, tell *Ladies' Home Journal* that she could now understand where feminists were coming from after her divorce.) Sociologist Amitai Etzioni said in 1977 that if the numbers progressed from where they stood, "not one American family" would be a traditional unit by the 1990s. When the National Organization for Women put almost all their efforts into adding the Equal Rights Amendment to the United States Constitution, Schlafly quickly "co-opted and misrepresented their arguments," effectively convincing herself and her following that the most important flaw in the women's movement was not its issues with intersectionality but that it was "anti-homemaker."

"Don't agonize, organize!" was the slogan created by Tish Sommers, a chair of the Task Force on Older Women within the National Organization for Women, for her campaign, which began in the 1970s, to help women find employment and support after a divorce. Influenced by her own background as a radical leftist organizer and the work of the International Wages for Housework Campaign, Sommers was a part of the second-wave feminist movement that located liberation in understanding the dynamics between race, age, class, and sexuality. Like Friedan's, Sommers's work would give a label to a predominant experience in individual women's lives that had no collective understanding. Like Friedan, she also downplayed her experience in grassroots left-wing political organizing; in the late 1930s, in fear of the spread of fascism, she had joined the Communist Party. She married another activist and they spent five years living "underground," organizing for civil rights with the Communist Party in the South. When she came to feminism in the 1960s, she saw racial inequality as the defining issue for the women's movement, and she spoke in 1970 about how the more time she spent within the movement, the deeper she was drawn into the issues of middle-class white women such as herself. That persona, in some ways, was a useful strategy: Levenstein identifies it as one that created an often-absent connection between the younger face of feminism and the older generations who didn't feel they had a reason to join, or a cause to participate in that served both them and their peers.

I doubt Schlafly would have been moved by the argument that there were elements of radical—even Marxist—analysis in

Sommers's displaced homemakers campaign. By attempting to place a monetary value on domestic labor, she was directly linking American economic power with the unpaid workforce handling the maintenance of individual shelters, the preparation of sustaining food, and the childcare of future generations.

Despite the reputation of alimony and spousal support (men's rights groups have often pointed to it as evidence that divorce is capable of bankrupting husbands, and detractors of no-fault divorce laws argued that without any punitive consequences for bad behavior women would be left destitute; Sommers's organizing partner, Laurie Shields, called it "legalized desertion"), it is not entirely common in practice, or at least not in the way it has been culturally understood—one of the many clichés about divorce that don't necessarily match the lived experience. In the 1970s in particular, Levenstein writes, the way judges interpreted alimony itself changed: previously the legal system had used alimony payments as something that committed ex-husbands to their former wives until those women remarried. Now it began to be seen as something more like a bridge between their time in the home and their time in the traditional workforce.

Before the 1970s, divorce proceedings focused on literal understandings of property and cash: anything owned and earned by a man usually was considered his alone, and ex-wives could expect, at maximum, about one third of that as their settlement. Throughout the 1970s and 1980s a new term took hold: *marital property*, which determined that such material elements belonged to each partner no matter who had made what. The family wage wasn't as strong as it once was, and judges took that into consideration. Women rarely received support for the rest of their lives, but the men's rights groups who had agitated for alimony's complete dissolution didn't win either.

In Sommers's work to achieve federal legislation solidifying some of these gains, Levenstein points to some much-needed perspective. This was the same era when Black, Latinx, Asian, and Indigenous feminist organizers were fighting against issues like police brutality, forced sterilization, and the devaluation and exploitation specific to their labor both inside and outside the home. The displaced homemakers movement did not have a meaningful contribution to make to these efforts, and more than that, as the backlash against so-called welfare queens grew in mainstream political discourse, they often actively withdrew from any explicitly anti-racist or anti-poverty organizing, positioning their supposed constituents as people more "deserving" of this assistance than others.

The postcolonial feminism theorist Chela Sandoval called this "hegemonic feminism," as Becky Thompson notes in her 2002 article, "Multiracial Feminism: Recasting the Chronology of Second Wave Feminism." The emphasis on Friedan and the cultural phenomenon that was *Mystique* ignores the work of women of color within organizations such as NOW, as well as within other radical or leftist organizations, and in tandem with organizations distinctly founded for the autonomy of women of color, by women of color. Sometimes there was overlap between such categories: the Third World Women's Alliance, for example, was founded in 1968 by members of the Student Nonviolent Coordinating Committee, and while the National Black Feminist Organization was only operational from 1973 to 1975, the members included people such as Florynce Kennedy, Michele Wallace, Barbara Smith, and Faith Ringgold; this, in turn, became part of the inspiration for the Combahee

River Collective. The concentric circles of anti-imperialism, anti-racism, anti–white supremacy, and queer liberation created more space and support for solidarity across common goals. It was Barbara Smith who said, "Feminism is the political theory and practice that struggles to free all women: women of color, working-class women, poor women, disabled women, lesbians, old women—as well as white, economically privileged, heterosexual women. Anything less than this vision of total freedom is not feminism, but merely female self-aggrandizement."

"The personal is political" is often referenced as the rallying call of second-wave feminism, but it was initially said by civil rights and Black Power activists, as well as student organizers; it was a well-used mantra before it became a popular motto and is usually sourced to an essay written by Carol Hanisch on the necessity and relevance of consciousness-raising groups; and possibly to Shulamith Firestone and Anne Koedt, who included it in an anthology they were editing, *Notes from the Second Year: Women's Liberation*. (The term *consciousness-raising* itself is credited to Kathie Sarachild, who had been a civil rights organizer in Mississippi and was also a founding member of both the Redstockings and New York Radical Women.) The anti-racist activist Anne Braden was the one who flipped it once again, into "The personal is political, and the political is personal."

In this way, people from all experiences were challenged to reconsider the boundaries they had once arbitrarily assigned to their own lives—to not assume that just because it wasn't their personal experience, it wasn't their political responsibility, and to not dismiss what happened in the minute corners of a life as somehow lesser to the cause. Audre Lorde once asked, in her speech "The Transformation of Silence into Language and Action," a question directly to white women: *are you doing your work?* These divides were painful—they still are today—and necessary. Sarah Schulman's book, *Conflict Is Not Abuse*, has many excellent points to make, but everything comes back to the power that exists in that four-word title: a conflict is not, in itself, an abuse.

Ms. magazine was one arena where those conflicts were often right on the surface. The publication, founded in 1971 and first published in 1972, had many critics who fairly considered the publication an unchallenged authority, co-opting grassroots organizing for a more palatable presentation in a nonprofit organization and a famously glamorous white woman leader, Gloria Steinem. Yet acknowledging those contradictions also became a strength (an echo of Jessie Bernard here: *Once we know enough to question cultural norms . . .*). In "Rejecting the Center: Radical Grassroots Politics in the 1970s," author Joshua Zeitz points out that it was only the most mainstream (and thus commercially appealing) of about two hundred feminist magazines currently in circulation. The first issue sold three hundred thousand copies in just over a week and received about twenty thousand letters to the editor. Within five years they had published essays that were still largely considered underground works, like a reprint of "The Myth of the Vaginal Orgasm," as well as the injustices faced by the wives of POWs in Vietnam. Advertiser surveys did show that the subscriber base was more diverse than that of any comparable title at the time: more people of color, and an even distribution between those of middle-class and working-class income levels, preferred to read *Ms.* There also was a small but significant percentage of readers who identified as men—just under 20 percent.

"One of the magazine's signature themes was the 'click' moment—the split second when a woman discovered her personal or economic subordination in a patriarchal world," writes Zeitz. One such example included a woman from South Carolina who described how she worked twelve-hour days in her family's business as well as maintained the household; she had been married for twenty-seven years, and always considered that normal. When, after reading *Ms.*, she decided to ask her husband why this was their dynamic, and suggested it was time for her to draw a paycheck from the business and start her own checking account, he refused. "He stated that since he was head of the household, these were privileges due him only," the reader said. "Click!" Zeitz follows this anecdote with the dry addendum: "The woman in question divorced her husband."

There were other, smaller print publications that didn't have to placate advertisers or balance other outside expectations. *Women: A Journal of Liberation* was one such publication, run by a feminist collective, and the winter 1971 edition was titled "The Family—How We Live and with Whom." The editorial opening the issue is about the ubiquity of the nuclear family: what they call a "microcosm of capitalist society as a whole," noting that out of the sixteen members who make up their staff, the majority do live in traditional structures, like the majority of America's women. Still, they believe it is possible to take out the hierarchy of such arrangements; to co-operate in groups, rather than possess and protect what amounts to a retreat from community. They acknowledge their own hesitation toward the idea of communal living—the issues dividing labor, both domestic and emotional, as well as the difficulty in finding people trustworthy enough to share a home with—but still hope it could prove a potential avenue to that promised liberation.

One particularly poignant section is an entry by Betsy Riley, who submits entries from the diary she kept from when she was a newlywed. Fourteen years have passed, and her annotation admits that she often lied, even if it was just for the pages she wrote to and about herself (and in case her husband did read it, which she says was likely). When they married, she assigned herself the role of caretaker: protecting her husband's writing by earning the majority of money for the household, and then doing all the housework. "Even after reading the diary over in retrospect," she says, "I cannot be sure how much my husband was to blame for the shitty situation we were in. I still feel ambivalent enough about my husband to want to believe that we were both potentially good human beings trapped in a horrendous romantic myth." In sharing these pages now, she says she "felt immense relief that I had survived all of those illusions about men and women and marriage."

An essay coauthored by Carol Scott and Jean Oken, "Divorce as Survival: The Buck Stops Here," encourages women not to fear divorce so much as to recognize that the fear is worth overcoming in order to survive a marriage that has become—or always was—oppressive. "We found that we didn't have to be very brave or strong or aggressive to get divorced," they write. "We just realized that our situation would destroy us if we remained in it. Making radical changes in the way we live thus becomes a simple act of self-preservation."

Scott and Oken warn that divorce lawyers are "disgusting men by and large," and that their technical skill is an unfortunate necessity but not a substitute for a source of approval. The stigma exists, both within the divorced women and in their social lives. "This alienation is real, and before we can get comfortable in a new environment it is necessary to relinquish our death-grip on the old one . . . we found that in doing the thinking that leads up to the decision to get divorced, we had already made a lot of changes in our values and priorities."

The essay ends with a statement, and another promise. "Possibly the greatest value in a divorce lies in the knowledge that our sins, our failings, our friends, our food, our vibes, our triumphs, our karma, our life is our doing and ours alone," they write, their belief in their own strength lifting off the page. "All responsibility, all criticism and all praise belong only to us."

I am most interested in stories about people who lived through—perhaps even can be credited as the architects of—real revolution, mostly because it reveals how no one knows that is what's happening in the moment itself. Their decisions and relationships and writings become a record of proof, yet when I read them now, I love them for their ambiguity. *Would* this work, they wonder, about their actions or their essays or any attempt they made to build something more than what was already familiar. Could it? Everything they made was just an offering, rather than an answer.

When Audre Lorde's divorce from Edwin Rollins was finalized in March 1975, her friends gave her a cake. The icing read *To Audre, the gay divorcee.*

Lorde did not write or speak much about her marriage to and subsequent divorce from Rollins, and the only interview Rollins ever gave about their marriage and divorce was to Alexis De Veaux for her 2006 biography of Lorde, *Warrior Poet.* The reporting offers a portrait of Lorde's life and her loves—the decisions she made, the beliefs she held, and the stories she would go on to write about how they all existed within her.

De Veaux writes that after seven years of marriage, Lorde was mostly silent about that time as well; they note that in the documentary *A Litany for Survival: The Life and Work of Audre Lorde,* the only comment the poet makes about Rollins is that he was the only man she ever considered marrying.

Lorde was introduced to Rollins by their mutual friend Margie Gumpert, as part of Gumpert's efforts to matchmake during a fundraising event for John F. Kennedy's presidential run. They had a lot in common, including, maybe most important, a small, close scene of friends in their late twenties and early thirties, from working-class families—"extremely intellectual, witty liberals," who, according to De Veaux, "considered themselves outcasts." Together they wanted more than the kind of life that was available: "They shared a dream of the country's political possibilities and experimented with visions of a new social order—one beyond racial and sexual boundaries . . . Within the group, the lines between heterosexuality, homosexuality, bisexuality, love, and friendship blurred. Irrespective of gender, sex between the friends was no secret." Lorde herself was having several overlapping affairs with two women and one man in this group. Apparently, Lorde and Rollins each later told Gumpert they were disappointed with the other, not seeing much of an attraction; they were also both having an affair with Gumpert at the time.

At thirty, Rollins had known for most of his life that he was attracted to men, and De Veaux describes what sounds like a compartmentalization to protect him from the judgment of his family. Eventually, this would turn into a secrecy that threatened real intimacy. Still, he was certain he wanted a family, and he became certain it should be with Lorde. She was reluctant, but not exactly opposed. After a trip to California and her participation in a protest against a civil defense drill, Lorde was developing her sense of adventure. The sixties had just started and the possibility of transformation was everywhere. Lorde was still hesitant about joining herself to a cause, but she was convincing herself more and more that she could, and should, commit to change, even revolution. She came home fatigued by casual relationships, and Rollins would visit often. She wasn't sold on him, even as a friend, though she did admit that she thought he was attractive. She liked his style, in conversation and in fashion—a lawyer who wore suits and glasses for work, he also had a reputation for his distinctly personal and elaborate sense of dress.

Lorde wasn't ready to commit, and he didn't want to have an affair. The longer they remained at this impasse, De Veaux writes, the closer Lorde got to changing her mind. Neither of them wanted a traditional marriage. They "both believed in the conventions of marriage and that they could raise children in a new kind of family. They were idealists, rebelling against mainstream norms." In November 1961, Rollins wrote her a long letter in which he tried to interrogate his own intentions: Was he lonely and ready for family, or was it something more? Was he forcing a relationship with her, a Black queer woman, to prove something about himself and his politics? The letter finished with a statement pledging emotions that were both "hopeful and genuine." He proposed on Christmas that same year. Audre deferred until morning, and then "grilled him on his sincerity, his intentions, testing his answers for signs of how deeply he'd thought; testing his resolve even further at one point by suggesting Ed didn't know what he was getting into." Was this kind of love enough to handle an entire marriage? To handle being a Black woman married to a white man, to prepare to have children together, right in the crux of a revolutionary civil rights movement?

None of her friends thought it was a good idea, and one ex-girlfriend even returned to offer to get back together instead of Lorde getting married. But Lorde didn't think her marriage was exactly opposed to her relationships with women. When she did agree to marry Rollins, it was under the condition that they would define their marriage on their own terms, without worrying about what other people thought. A friend who attended their wedding asked Lorde if they had invited every woman Lorde had ever slept with. Lorde told her: "It looks like it." For their honeymoon, they stayed at her apartment, took the phone off the hook, and rented cars to drive to different beaches around New York.

Lorde started the decade known for enormous social change as a married woman in a heterosexual union. In her essay "Learning from the 60s," she wrote that the decade was marked, for her, in justifications: she was asked to "justify my existence and my work, because I was a woman, because I was a Lesbian, because I was not a separatist, because some piece of me was not acceptable. Not because of my work but because of my identity."

These justifications often caused her some pain. A reverend named Sofeld asked to meet her because he had been assigned to write about a Black author of his choosing. She liked meeting him and gave him all her old poems to read for his research. But when she read the finished paper, she was so, so hurt. Sofeld wrote that he wondered where "the early promise of this bright, talented poet" had gone. "Look at her now," he wrote, "married, with children, and no new poems in the last two years. What a shame." Lorde feared his words, and the judgment they contained. She was only thirty-three years old; was this it for her, and her poetry?

Her time at Tougaloo College in Jackson, Mississippi, is of a similar emotional tenor, and well-known to her devoted readers. In 1968 Lorde went to Tougaloo as their poet-in-residence, and when she met the students in her poetry workshop, she "dreaded the vulnerability of any exposure she did not initiate," and so chose to tell them directly that she was married to a white man, and had two children with him. She didn't get into the problems present in their marriage; instead, she advocated not for the marriage itself but for her right to choose her own commitments, no matter what sort of sociopolitical conventions she knew existed. This was a disclosure that would ultimately expand the way she and her students spoke about civil rights and anti-Black racism into lived experiences rather than pure theory.

Lorde's book *Sister Outsider* includes an interview with her close friend and frequent collaborator, the poet Adrienne Rich, in which Lorde does comment on her marriage. She speaks about it deeply, if briefly. Rich mentions how hard defending the marriage must have been on theoretical terms, when in real life, it was "going nowhere. It's like having to defend something that was not in itself defensible," she says. Lorde responds, "What I was defending was something that needed defense. And this moved it out of 'I'm defending Ed because I want to live with him.' It was, 'I'm defending this relationship because we have a right to examine it and try it.'"

Still, she felt the contradictions, and knew that the right to examine and try could only take her so far. She talks about how difficult it was to defend her choices, to be starting a relationship with a woman, Frances Clayton, and at the same time trying to deal with "what was going on with this insane man I lived with who wanted to continue pretending life could be looked at one way and lived another."

Many years later Lorde would tell her daughter, Beth, that the marriage had worked for the time that it did because it was open to what they called "loving friends," but their commitment was always to the marriage first. When Lorde did fall in love with Clayton, who would turn out to be the defining relationship of her life, she felt it constituted an emotional infidelity that deserved their full attention. She wanted to go to couples therapy; Rollins wanted to let things continue as they were. By the time they did separate their distance had grown into a mixture of hostility and bitterness. Lorde was excited by the idea of reinvention, the possibility of living fully as a lesbian, famously writing in her journal that she was "lustful now for my own name." But she also mourned the marriage and struggled with Rollins's claims to custody. By 1971 they had finalized a separation agreement that included a clause forbidding Lorde to take their two children to live out of New York State, obviously intended to prevent her from moving to Rhode Island and living with Clayton. Lorde officially came out in 1973 during a reading at a bookstore and coffee shop on West Seventy-Second street, to a packed house that included Adrienne Rich. She read "Love Poem," which had been rejected the first time she submitted it because the editor had objected to the use of female pronouns. Rich remembered it as a "staggering moment" for her, as she was also in the process of coming out. "Love Poem" later appeared in the February 1974 edition of *Ms.* magazine.

The divorce was finalized on March 21, 1975, because of "irreconcilable differences." Lorde's divorce papers stated that she could return to her maiden name, something she had insisted on, and after that she would always be cited and credited as Audre Lorde. Lorde and Rollins's relationship remained contentious, and he was often late with child support. Lorde took him to court and won, and he was angry enough at her to stop speaking to their children, having almost no contact with them between 1976 and 1978. Eventually they found some peace as a family. Lorde's relationship with Clayton was not some idyllic fairy tale either—they had their own issues with dependency, monogamy, and parenting—yet understanding this era of her life as part of her work seems to be entirely the point. The prisms of her experience reveal so much. The ways she once denied herself became the ways she knew herself; they are the ways that can show how she became herself.

In one of her most well-known essays, "Uses of the Erotic," she writes of how hard it is to have and to share an "erotic charge" in her time. "I know it was not available to me when I was trying to adapt my consciousness to this mode of living and sensation," she writes. But to acknowledge and see that power of the erotic—and with it, everything else her definition of the concept encompassed, like romance and sensuality and electricity—would give "the energy to pursue genuine change within our world, rather than merely settling for a shift of characters in the same weary drama." It is a choice never finished being made; what Lorde conjures as a "longed-for bed which I enter gratefully and from which I rise up empowered."

Here is a partial reading list of books my friends warned me to avoid in the first year of my divorce: *Aftermath* by Rachel Cusk. *Dept. of Speculation* by Jenny Offill. *See Now Then* by Jamaica Kincaid. They would just make me cry, they said. I read them anyway—spitefully, hopefully. I rejected my friends' concern because I thought maybe it would be cathartic, but nothing worked. "That seems right," I would say out loud, alone, turning the pages with my heart level and my eyes dry. I often used, as a response, a screenshot of a photo saved on my phone that my friends and I loved: paparazzi photographs of Nicole Kidman exuberantly walking down what might be an alleyway or parking lot, taken after she had apparently finalized her divorce from Tom Cruise, her face pained and relieved, sometimes her head thrown back and her hands in the air. The contradictions of her expressions said a lot more than I could have.

The friend who warned me not to read *Dept. of Speculation* is a longtime newspaper editor, and one time I watched her carefully correct a class of journalism students. One of them had presented a pitch that was incomplete and poorly formed, but not without merit. "That's a subject," she said as a way to explain what was lacking. "It's not a story."

What was divorce to me? The subject, or the story?

A young woman has started sleeping in the spare bedroom of a vacation home shared by two families. Among them is a fairly famous poet, and the young woman is more than a fan. She believes they have to meet and feels entitled to what he can give her. The poet is more confused than afraid. His wife understands more than she lets on. Their teenage daughter, watching how a group of people can cause or affect an atmosphere, is witness to more than anyone knows. Each character in this novel is fated for something, but whether anyone is aware of the aura of humid dread that hangs over their dinner scenes is unclear. The tension builds and builds past the point when it feels like it should break.

Swimming Home, by Deborah Levy, is a dream: words become images that sink to the bottom of your subconscious. The story makes sense in the moment, but upon recollection becomes hazy. In one scene, a knife hovers a centimeter away from a pearl necklace—the image seems more important in memory than in relation to the plot. All the characters serve their purpose, no matter how brief, but their entrances and exits are so slow one can never be sure if they are coming or going. There is blood everywhere, but very little violence. The sex is so sexy, but there is almost no fucking. The novel kept me awake one long night and stayed with me through the next morning. I loved it.

Lots of people did: *Swimming Home* was shortlisted for the Man Booker Prize in 2012. Critics praised Levy's fiction as graceful and lurid, cerebral and simple. But praise doesn't pay the bills. "One afternoon, I made my way from the writing shed to a meeting about a possible film option on one of my novels," writes Levy in *The Cost of Living*, her 2018 memoir that is the second in a trilogy of recent books about her life. She has ridden her bike to meet with film executives who wonder if *Swimming Home* could be made into a movie.

This meeting matters a lot: it must go well; she cannot be late. Levy is recently divorced, living with her teenage daughters, and trying her best to support them on a writer's income. Her daughters need money for school, her gas bill needs to be paid, and most horrifying of all are the noises her laptop has started to make. When the executives ask her an important question, she concentrates on it: Who is the main character of her novel? Is it the poet, whom she has named Jozef Nowogrodzki? Or Kitty Finch, the woman who could be his lover, stalker, or protégé? Levy pitches herself as the writer of the screenplay, assuring them she can handle the looping approach to linear time, the conflicting readings of the people she's invented. The executives are not convinced.

No one can fault the film executives for their hesitation. Scenes that make the book beautiful to read contain elements that might seem hard to convey visually, and Levy's characters inspire a lot of questions. Kitty Finch is introduced swimming naked in the pool of the vacation home in the South of France, and it is obvious that her character is there to seduce. Yet when she opens her mouth to speak she surprises everyone with a pronounced speech impediment. Do sirens stutter? Jozef Nowogrodzki, the writer Kitty has come for, is called Joe by his readers, who number enough to make him, we're told, famous and rich. He's described as charismatic, alluring. Can poets be handsome? After the meeting, Levy looks in a mirror and sees something in her reflection. Does she have leaves in her hair? In a daydream, she imagines a future version of herself living like some kind of Robert Evans figure, "a legendary sun-damaged genius of cinema." Meanwhile, in present-day London, she has to bike her groceries for dinner back home in the rain.

The three memoirs, starting with *Things I Don't Want to Know* in 2013 and ending with *Real Estate* in 2021, are Levy's life story—brief interludes about the days that compose the decades. Her divorce has already happened; so has her childhood. Now comes everything else, ordinary or otherwise.

The first of the trilogy is *Things I Don't Want to Know*, and the two that follow maintain the same laconic elegance she sets as tone. There is something to the way Levy writes that makes one believe she could hear, see, read, or experience anything and say, *OK.* She offers many interpretations, but few judgments and even fewer conclusions. Her loyalties are total and her betrayals are final. She accepts the people in her life as they are, not as she wishes them to be; she grieves her losses and lets them go. When her groceries fall out of her e-bike basket and a car drives over the chicken she had planned to make for dinner, she roasts it anyway. When her mother dies, she lets her memories overtake her as they come, and then brings herself back. In one scene in *Cost*, she tells a friend of a friend that she considers nostalgia a waste of time—a pretty funny thing to say for someone writing a three-volume autobiography.

But then nostalgia and reflection are not necessarily the same thing. "I have never wanted to cover the past in dust sheets to preserve it from change," she explains. It's hard enough to live a life, let alone write it down—hard enough, as she tells us, to be a woman alone, a woman of a certain age. Levy keeps these thoughts to herself not because there is nothing to say, but because there are so many ways to answer the question she remembers being asked—"You're a writer, aren't you?"—and so few words that fit. Who is the main character of the writing she's doing here? Can an author ever really be the main character of their own book when the reader is right there, looking for themselves?

After her divorce, Levy moves her children into an apartment where something is always breaking down or going wrong. Everything needs a repair; every fix has a price. "Freedom is never free," she writes. "Anyone who has struggled to be free knows how much it costs." She tries to fix the plumbing herself, tries to find time and space to write. A longtime friend, Celia, offers her garden shed as a shelter for her work, and guards it for Levy like a fortress. In that tiny room, made cozy by various accessories she brings back from her travels or domestic impulsive purchases, Levy writes many books—the books that win awards, get her the meetings with the movie executives. She writes the book we hold in our hands, she tells us, not to turn these pages into a trophy, but to account for how they came to exist at all. She wears pearls while she works. Celia, who loves her and makes her work possible, can't wrap her head around the pearls. *Pearls?* Levy overhears her saying to a friend. *Just to write in a dusty old shed?*

There is no immediate offering to make sense of what could be metaphor, no answer to the implied questions: *What do the pearls mean? What do they mean here?* But this is what makes Levy's writing the pleasure it is: her understanding that she is, whether author or subject, required to be a character. In a novel, a writer must prove to us they know what everyone is thinking. In a memoir, a writer must admit they barely know what they're thinking, let alone anyone else's thoughts. Levy knows we know that ideas must come from somewhere. Like a pearl necklace, the way a writer turns thoughts into a sequence that suits is nothing short of a miracle. *How did you find so many that fit together?* I thought as I read these brief passages that add up to the impression that I am reading if not the whole story, then certainly the parts that matter most. I know the answer. With luck, and a lot of equipment.

The ghosts of past and future are major characters in Levy's works. Herself as a child; her mother, recently deceased; the woman she was before she had children; the woman she was when she was a wife. In *Real Estate*, she finds a book her ex-husband had inscribed in 1999, when they were still married. "To my Darling love for last Christmas of the Century with 1000 years of devotion," he had promised. "I tried to connect with Her (who is my younger self), to remember how she had responded to this gift at the time," Levy writes.

"I did not want to see her too clearly. But I did try to wave to her. I knew she would not want to see me (*so there you are, nearly sixty and alone*) and I did not want to see her either (*so there you are, forty years old, hiding your talent, trying to keep your family together*), but she and I haunted each other across time."

Sometimes she mentions her muses—Marguerite Duras, Virginia Woolf, Simone de Beauvoir, James Baldwin, Elizabeth Hardwick, Jean Genet—as though they hover around us, waiting for us to start an imaginary conversation or pick a semi-hallucinated fight. Hardwick, a complicated favorite, is especially important. In her novel *Sleepless Nights*, the narrator occasionally turns over her decision to include details about an unnamed husband, taking inventory of what she needs to have or wants to know. Hardwick wrote *Nights* soon after her estranged husband, the poet Robert Lowell, died; soon, too, after he had published a book of poems called *The Dolphin* that used Hardwick's correspondence about their separation and his new relationship as material. The associative style in Hardwick's writing, rather than the details, is the point: the letters to friends, anecdotes about roommates, and vignettes describing evenings spent at home add up to something better felt than known. Hardwick began drafting the book under the title *The Cost of Living*.

Levy's whole project of her memoirs may have ended up far from where she started, but it does have a point of origin: the classic essay by George Orwell, "Why I Write," was the inspiration for *Things I Don't Want To Know*. Like many writers who reference this work, the why evaporates almost instantly. This is because, as a question, why one writes has a pretty boring answer: for love or money. There are nuances, I'm sure, and often some deeper context. There are degrees of affection, and fluctuations of currency. But examining all of that closely gets old fast.

Orwell believed his most lifeless books were the ones that lacked political purpose, which led to "sentences without meaning, decorative adjectives and humbug generally." Perhaps this is what tethers the love to money. To him, political purpose was one of the four reasons for writing that went beyond making money, along with ego and ambition, a historical impulse (the "desire to see things as they are, to find out true facts and store them up for the use of posterity"), and aesthetics—the perception of beauty and the right words to convey it, or the arrangement of words on the page; the pleasure of rhythm, or of telling a really good story to a person who really wants to hear it. "The aesthetic motive is very feeble in a lot of writers, but even a pamphleteer or writer of textbooks will have pet words and phrases which appeal to him for non-utilitarian reasons," he writes. "Above the level of a railway guide, no book is quite free from aesthetic considerations."

Levy's writing is beautiful, but that's not just what it is. Her subject *is* beauty—the things that we cannot look away from. "There is something about beauty, really extreme beauty, that I think is quite freakish," she said in a 2019 CBC interview, as part of her press tour for *The Man Who Saw Everything*, her eighth novel. "We want to stare at beauty, but decorum tells us that we have to avert our eyes. When we're in love with someone and want to look at them, we don't want to be caught doing that because it is not very cool. But we do want to look." In this interview she talks about loving pearls because they hold the heat of the body.

"Everything was calm," writes Levy at the start of *Cost*. Her marriage, described as being like a boat anchored close to where she is swimming, is placid under a bright sun. "Then, when I surfaced twenty years later, I discovered there was a storm, a whirlpool, a blasting gale lifting the waves over my head. At first I wasn't sure I'd make it back to the boat and then I realized I didn't want to make it back to the boat.

"My marriage was the boat and I knew that if I swam back to it, I would drown," Levy continues, in the paragraph I think about most often. "It is also the ghost that will always haunt my life. I will never stop grieving for my long-held wish for enduring love that does not reduce its major players to something less than they are. I am not sure I have often witnessed love that achieves all of these things, so perhaps this ideal is fated to be a phantom. What sort of questions does this phantom ask of me? It asks political questions for sure, but it is not a politician."

Everything ends. Perhaps I am responding to what I often consider the reassuring bluntness of describing everything that happens after what other books or lives might consider the last chapter—in this case, a divorce. I, personally, like to have reminders that I've changed my life before and can do it again. I might make it worse—again—but I can definitely change it. *There was a storm.* But when I picture happiness, half-awake and pretending I'm only dreaming, I still want what I want: to believe I am living a life without interruption.

This is the sum of an inheritance that Levy references—the price writers pay while writing is a mix of odd luxuries and frequent asceticism, an accounting that never quite manages to balance. At one point, she recognizes that de Beauvoir may not be aware of her influence on Levy's life or respect the choices she has made. "She was my muse," she writes, "but I was certainly not hers." Ghosts and muses do have a lot in common, I realized as I read through Levy's scenes. They don't seem to get to choose who sees them.

There is a living ghost that haunts memoirs by and about divorced women, and her name is Elizabeth Gilbert. In the first part of the story of her life, Gilbert wrote fiction and essays; she and Norman Mailer are reportedly the only unpublished writers to have ever had a short story submitted to and selected from the slush pile of *Esquire* magazine. In 1993, "Pilgrims" appeared under the headline "The Debut of an American Writer." Gilbert was twenty-four.

The work she got following her debut, for magazines like *GQ*, *Spin*, and *The New York Times Magazine*, took her all over the world, and like the hero of a florid romance, that was where she felt most herself. One essay recounted her time working in a dive bar with a devoted following, and it was adapted into the 2000 film *Coyote Ugly*. The story changed drastically, but the ending was somewhat the same: Gilbert, and her fictional proxy, in love with a man she met over the course of her time working there. For the real woman, that man would become her husband, and her now well-established career was supporting their married life, until she realized at age thirty that she did not want to be married at all.

The plot of the memoir that followed this revelation begins with Gilbert weeping on the floor of the bathroom, begging for an answer as to why she could not want the life she had. She ultimately decided to divorce her husband soon after a man she met on assignment in Bali predicted that she would lose all her money once in her life but then get it right back. The loss would turn out to be the settlement in her divorce, and the return would be the advance for *Eat Pray Love*, an idea she sold to her publisher on a proposal to travel to Italy, India, and Indonesia, devoting herself entirely to what she deemed the most essential qualities of each location: pleasure in Italy, faith in India, healing in Indonesia. At the end she meets the man who will become a great love of her life.

Gilbert's blockbuster memoir was not the first work in which a divorced woman finds a way back to material or emotional wealth following the end of her marriage. But it has come to represent a popular idea: that with the right new landscape and new wardrobe and maybe new spiritual practice (and definitely a new love interest), divorce can be a journey in itself, not unlike its literary predecessor and contemporary companion, the marriage plot. To date *Eat Pray Love* has, according to Gilbert, sold over twelve million copies worldwide, a work of such cultural significance that its impact and influence outshine, perhaps, the actual fact of reading the book.

Gilbert would eventually (like the Cher adage that periodically resurfaces and recirculates on social media, about how she had to tell her mother she didn't need to marry a rich man because she was a rich man) stop looking for a guru to follow and instead be the guru herself. With the boost that follows most of the charismatic guests who appeared on *The Oprah Winfrey Show* during its run on daytime television, her audience began to develop from readers to followers. In 2015, Gilbert published *Big Magic: Creative Living Beyond Fear*, a self-help book in the same vein as *The Artist's Way* by Julia Cameron and *The Writing Life* by Annie Dillard: authors encouraging creativity with varying spiritual influences. Gilbert's advice is to think of ideas as a singular element of our universe, in the same way oxygen and water circulate far and wide—that an idea is out there searching for someone who breathes it in and makes it real. *Eat Pray Love*, she writes, was hardly an original idea; lots of people want to leave their marriages and travel far away to explore their different interests. "I cannot tell you (it is literally beyond my ability to count) how many people have accused me in anger of having written their book," she recounts. (Some people have just made their peace with feeling this way by writing it anyway—that's the idea behind *Eat Pray Love Made Me Do It*, an essay collection published in 2016 that has an introduction from Gilbert but is otherwise entirely about other people's experiences of reading and relating to the book.) "But what can I say?" Gilbert defers. "What do I know about that stranger's life? From my perspective, I found an unattended idea lying around, and I ran away with it." *Eat Pray Love* was no longer a memoir she had written to financially support herself. Instead it became "a huge screen upon which millions of people projected their most intense emotions."

Even if *Eat Pray Love* did not invent a genre, the success of the book and its film adaptation has made Gilbert's divorce memoir a standard within a canon. It is now a trope of literature by divorced women to see many kinds of diaries laid over one another—travel, money, food. We expect them to always be jetting off to European countries, to bite into a fruit of the season and find it perfectly ripe. (The success of the film adaptation of *Under the Tuscan Sun*, in which Diane Lane plays a recently divorced writer and professor who moves to Italy and undertakes a charmingly frustrating process of renovating a gorgeous house, is both inspired by and an inspiration for at least some of the "rustic Tuscan" aesthetic resurgence in interior design and food trends, such as sun-dried tomatoes.) Divorced women are allowed a little decadence in these books, even encouraged to try it. There is a seductiveness to their movements, one that casts differently depending on how they might already be seen. Should the divorcée be sad and mournful, or relieved and rapturous? A certain amount of voluntary celibacy ensures that all the eroticism she experiences happens outside of sex. Many of them also share the same class subconsciousness—an awareness of what their status was and what it could become is both the subject and the subtext of their writing. One doesn't have to read Jane Austen to know that, just like marriage, divorce can be a significant determiner of an adult person's financial position.

Not unlike the way tote bags and journals and other merchandise that capitalize on Virginia Woolf's famous sentence about a woman writer needing a room of her own but then forget to include the part about how women also need money—"five hundred pounds a year," approximately forty thousand American dollars today, and also a lock on that door—Gilbert's reasons for writing the book are often remembered more as a form of liberation than income. But the prophecy that led her back to Bali wasn't just about leaving her marriage; it was the certainty that in doing so she would lose all the money she had made up until that point, along with the property that money had bought. Because Gilbert does not share the exact details (and because to a certain extent those details don't matter), speculation is irrelevant, though it's worth noting that she makes a quip warning readers not to divorce in New York. At the time of her divorce, New York State had not yet adopted no-fault divorce laws, meaning that whichever party was found to be the cause of the marital dissolution would have incurred a harsh financial penalty; there are allusions to spousal support even in her follow-up memoir, published four years after *Eat*, and other expenses that would explain how and why temporary rentals might be more practical than attempting to sign a lease. She bluntly mentions that the advance for the book is how she paid for the time spent writing it.

"Readers have opened their hearts to Gilbert's message of finding happiness within themselves—but will they also open their wallets?" asked ABC News in 2010, reporting that over four hundred products based on the themes of *Eat Pray Love* would be up for sale in tandem with the film's release. There was "Italian, Indian and Indonesian-themed merchandise so consumers can have their own—albeit less dramatic—'Eat Pray Love' experiences." The Home Shopping Network, as part of a partnership with Sony, programmed seventy-two straight hours of *Eat Pray Love*–related merchandise, like a $350 prayer bead necklace. Fresh, a line of skincare and beauty products, released their own *Eat Pray Love* line inspired by its "journey for the senses," while Lancôme sold a set of their cult classic Juicy Tubes lip gloss branded as special *Eat Pray Love* colors. There was jewelry and limited-edition teas. There was even a Spirit Quest Tours vacation package to Bali where, for twenty-four hundred American dollars, they would include a visit with Gilbert's teacher, Ketut Liyer, and her friend from the book, Wayan.

Gilbert is estimated to have received $1 million for the film rights, and approximately $10 million in royalties from the book at the time of the film's release. Some of that money, she told *The New York Times*, went to renovating a store she owned with her then-husband: "This should be called the Julia Roberts Memorial Building," she joked when they visited it in 2010.

No one could miss the paradox that comes with selling merchandise to celebrate a book about a woman who finds herself after she leaves behind everything she's ever made or owned. Elizabeth Wellington, for *The Philadelphia Inquirer*, wrote that *Eat* was a very personal story about a very deep depression: what Gilbert did not do to heal herself was "rock Dana Buchman tunics or light Yankee candles in her room at the ashram as Kohl's is trying to get us to do." Joshunda Sanders and Diana Barnes-Brown critiqued this phenomenon in *Bitch* magazine, calling the genre of books that *Eat Pray Love* and other comparable titles from Oprah's Book Club belong to "priv-lit": a proliferation of media aimed at celebrating women's hard-won and, in many cases, negligible economic gains by encouraging them to spend everything they had on making themselves better. "The book could easily have been called *Wealthy, Whiny, White*," the authors say. "*Eat Pray Love* and its position as an Everywoman's guide to whole, empowered living embody a literature of privilege and typify the genre's destructive cacophony of insecurity, spending, and false wellness."

Gilbert's follow-up to *Eat Pray Love* is titled *Committed: A Love Story*, and it poses a much different story than her memoir of divorce and independence: it's about getting married. The ending of *Eat Pray Love* had the soft lens of a romance, the quintessential bow wrapping around a neat finality. Now the story continued with Gilbert's rather desperate inquiries into the entire history of marriage, explained as originating from the Department of Homeland Security's decision to ban her partner from continuing to visit the United States on tourist visas.

Gilbert adopts the same charmed, bewildered tone of the classic magazine essay—anecdotal digressions, colorful details, surprising characters, and a light peppering of statistics and facts—and while much of it is pretty charming, much more of it seems pleading. There is an unrequited quality to both books, a call to the reader that can't, by virtue of the way reading works, really be answered: an ask for permission, maybe, or even forgiveness.

In the tenth-anniversary edition of *Eat Pray Love*, Gilbert's introduction contains a much-welcomed sense of perspective. "People sometimes make fun of this book," she acknowledges. "Sometimes I make fun of it. Sincere as she was, its author is terribly earnest and occasionally grandiose." She recognizes how odd it was for her to spend so much time fixated on her age (she was in her early thirties, which is not so much relatively young as actually young), the privilege of that advance coming right as she lost her savings, and that she had the flexibility to leave her life behind and trust that what mattered would wait for her to return. But in rereading for this anniversary edition, Gilbert says with a degree of self-compassion that is often absent from the original text, she realized the only reason she had that freedom was because she was a mess. Her bravado and her humor on the page often feel forced, weighted with much too heavy intentions: to explain, to understand, to request and receive forgiveness. But the reader can't give her that. The reader doesn't even know the depth of loss beyond the glib jokes about divorce law and rhapsodies about meditation. "It was easy for me to leave everything behind because I didn't have much to leave behind," she writes. "I had no property, because I'd lost it all in my divorce. I had no romantic relationships, because I'd exploded them. I had no job, because I'd quit it. Everything was in turmoil, everything was in flux and I was so bloody sad. I had forgotten how sad I was."

That is the other quality missed in remembering the impact *Eat*

Pray Love had on divorce narratives—that the sadness came through in short scenes, moments of tears with new friends or in transcendent closure experienced in meditation, but everything about it was sad. Even as she writes about this determined search for pleasure in Italy and peace throughout India and Indonesia, the guilt and the loneliness drive her jokes about being too talkative at the ashram, or sustaining a prolonged period of abstinence, or eating what is most likely the very best slice of pizza in the whole wide world.

The idea of what a woman might have paid to get rid of the label of *wife*, or what it might have cost, is a story much richer in the imagination than it is in the details. In all these ways Deborah Levy remains close to the type that Gilbert exemplified, or perhaps compartmentalized, in that canon of literature by divorced women. ("Sometimes I would sprinkle sea salt on a wedge of sour green tomato and dip it into the peppery emerald olive oil," Levy writes in *Real Estate*, making groceries into treasures.) But what isn't clichéd when we're dealing with the totems of an institution—itself deeply unoriginal—that has never quite lost its power on even those who claim to be enlightened beyond it?

Levy's last installment of her memoirs is her empty-nest book, where she quotes Gaston Bachelard's *The Poetics of Space* as a way of explaining the passages where her daydreams take us. "If one were to give an account of all the doors one has closed and opened, of all the doors one would like to re-open," Bachelard wrote, "one would have to tell the story of one's entire life." The doors Levy has closed behind her don't seem to bother her as much as the doors she deliberately dreams of opening. The desire for another door to open seems to express more than her taste. She is paused between thresholds.

I was married on a cold day in December in my mother-in-law's living room. Our friends made the food; my new sister-in-law—real sisters now, we agreed, after so many years of just acting like it—plugged in her karaoke machine. I answered the door to about fifty guests, their entry without ceremony and full up on love. Everyone who attended was someone close to us, with a few exceptions for last-minute guests that I felt especially warm toward in the moment. Though we hadn't made any plans beyond where we'd be, what we'd wear, and what everyone should eat, our friends refused to be just guests: they orchestrated speeches and brought decorations, and one group of my coworkers from the clothing boutique I worked at then even rented a limousine, pulling up to the small driveway with the sunroof open and making everyone's jaws drop. "Those are Haley's fashion friends," a friend of mine confidently explained to a family member.

After enough time had passed, friends stopped warning me away from books about divorce and instead made sure to text me every time they encountered something that seemed designed for my interest in the topic. I received a double-digit number of texts when *The New York Review of Books* reissued *Divorcing*, Susan Taubes's hallucinatory novel about the end of a marriage and a court battle that turns into a funeral procession. The writing has the same surreal feeling of a particularly potent nightmare, the kind that feels like your subconscious has some vendetta to enact against you and will not rest until you cannot rest.

I became very jealous whenever I remembered a sentence Joan Didion wrote for the column she used to publish in *Life* magazine. She and her husband were not doing well, but they were in Honolulu. "We are here on this island in the middle of the Pacific in lieu of filing for divorce," she reported. How elegant, to leave it at that. How maddening.

When the column was published her friends and her husbands' friends all called in concerned panics, and she reportedly reassured or deflected them, defending herself by explaining: "In lieu! I said in lieu of!"

Sometime in the summer of 1973, Adrienne Rich sent a short letter to Elizabeth Hardwick. "Dearest E," she began, "I'm still feeling bloodyminded about those poems." Rich was a good friend of Robert Lowell, Hardwick's then-estranged husband, and she was blunt with him in private and in public about what she read in his book of poems, *The Dolphin.* "What does one say about a poet who, having left his wife and daughter for another marriage, then titles a book with their names, and goes on to appropriate his ex-wife's letters written under stress and pain of desertion, into a book of poems nominally addressed to the new wife?" Rich wrote in *The American Poetry Review,* before revealing that she had a suggestion of her own: "I have to say that I think this is bullshit eloquence."

The remainder of her letter to Hardwick reads: "When 2 people have had something together, however difficult & painful, it is not the right of one to choose to 'use' it in this fashion. I think people are ultimately more important than poems (I know you do too!)."

To Lowell, she wrote just as bluntly. A thread of toughness reads between her notes about how much she cared for him, how it pained her to think of them growing apart, but that she must say what she thought about what he wrote. She was not just a good friend of Lowell's, but maybe in this harshness she was also a good friend *to* him, a distinction worth considering. In reading letters and published works, there is a form of love here—a reminder that critique can be done with great care, even when the pages radiate with hurt.

Like a dedication to the genre, the divorce memoir reenacts its own reason for existing: publishing one breaks hearts. When we read a divorce memoir and look for ourselves within it, the choice of who to relate to will change depending on where—not who—we are. What role do readers play in this exchange? Because the divorce memoir is neither a confessional nor a conversation, its writers have to play by ear: How will this sound? How will it echo back to me? When we place ourselves in the reader's position, are we making ourselves into the author, collecting our thoughts into sentences and our sentences into a story? Are we the anonymized ex, measuring our opportunities for rebuttal? Or are we the friend—the Adrienne Rich—waiting for the moment to say what we really think, and hoping it finds space in someone's consciousness?

The divorce plot, if such a thing can be said to exist, resists the contemporary facts of divorce: even if anyone can and does hold the capacity to end a marriage, it is still rarer to find a protagonist who is the one who leaves rather than the one who is left. Just the fact of a divorce can already inspire a recoil, and it is a brave person who will confront this assumption deliberately rather than avoid it indefinitely. What are the terms that must be met in order to write about one's divorce with beauty and respect? Asking the writer will be a very different experience compared to asking their ex.

In an earlier letter to Lowell, Rich had said that her memories of her friendship with him and Hardwick during their marriage were some of her happiest, most cherished. She loves remembering them as they were as a couple. Still, she doesn't mourn the change, exactly.

She admires, she says, who Hardwick is becoming. "Women are more interesting now than they've ever been, and even women like E. who were always interesting have become more subtle, more searching," she contemplates. "So many of us through one thing or another—choice, divorce, suicide or death, chance of some kind—are living more autonomous lives, and it's like a second youth, only with far more sense of direction, of one's real needs and longings, as opposed to the heady confusion of first youth." Is she right? Can an experience like divorce, and the decision to live not only through it but also beyond it, inspire not just a graceful ending but something actually new? Can we find that quality in our days, then recognize it in what we read and, finally, create it all over again in our own words?

The more I read and watched, the more I wondered what I was doing. What did I need from these stories, or more to the point, what was I avoiding? What feeling or action did they allow me to replace? I believed everything I saw, even though I knew it wasn't real, or even meant to be interpreted as real. I had a precipitous gullibility that I indulged, allowing myself a passive but committed dive headfirst into a narrative, or a character, or an end. No matter how often these concepts disappointed me by being exactly what they were (narrow, for one; embarrassing as a posture to adopt in real life, for another), I still held out a little hope. Maybe I just hadn't found the right one yet.

In lots of fiction, divorce is not so much a genre as it is an event. Ending a marriage can be a plot point in a tragedy or farce or any combination of the qualities that make both; it can be romantic or dramatic, tearful or a celebration. On the other hand, there is clearly a small yet prominent kind of divorce narrative that could be called its own genre. The conventional marriage plot reminds us that love stories end with a wedding. Heartbreak stories have slightly more flexibility. They can begin or end with a divorce, or the question of separation can be the conflict that drives the entire story. But I do think that over time a clearer pattern emerges, one that intertwines the question of whether people define the law or the law defines people. Traveling backward from Levy and Gilbert, the contemporaries of divorce writing, to the gossipy novels of the 1970s and the bleak suburban despair of 1950s novels, I sense something that connects them together. I see the same in the glossiness of modern divorce movies that come alongside the pained dramas that reference custody battles or infidelities or other betrayals, to the grainy film stock of auteurs and independents, to the stark black-and-white depictions of toothy dialogue in the comedies of remarriage or the grayscale yearnings of Hays Code–era melodramas. It is a genre that knows blame without fully accepting it, a fiction that says: you cannot possibly fault me for telling you this, because either I have been honest or I have been right.

It is, as with any rule, easy enough to find exceptions, and there are many. Still, even the variations follow their own version. Gilbert's writing is where I first started testing out my theory like a science experiment, and began to see how it was not just her *Eat Pray Love* journey that served as an inspiration and lodestar for the genre. It was also in the sunny evasion of the real story, the one she later reflected on as barely hiding her deep sadness and fear. To tell a divorce story, from start to finish, is beyond betrayal. It would be its own form of infidelity—the breaking of a promise made in marriage that carries well past divorce. Every writer who cares about goodness not just as a form of craft but as a principle relies on the same technique: a shading of the borders around the story, a writing or expression that gives depth to the details, sensations, and emotions of an experience as an exchange instead of saying what really happened.

In novels, like Jamaica Kincaid's *See Now Then* and Jenny Offill's *Speculation*, there is a great sense of truth and honesty with narrators who can see the entire scope of the story and characters who can show their thoughts, and the distance between the writer and the book allows the reader the space to put in their own specifics; there are moments when one character is clearly at fault and others when the decision to leave is clear. Still, the dissolution of marriage doesn't come easily or obviously. Sacrifices to fairness must be made. In the nonfiction of writers like Cheryl Strayed and Rachel Cusk—people who have, through the force of their thinking and writing, made room for ambiguities in all scales of human emotion—there is also a limit to what they'll say about their former partners, an opaqueness that offers the most cutting of insights and understandings without giving away how they learned it. After all, they are under no obligation to teach us anything, or to help us, any more so than any other kind of literature is. (A friend of mine, when we were discussing this trend toward looking to divorce memoirs for guidance, joked with devastating insight: Must every book we read become self-help?) Even in the singular nature of a writer assured of her own style, and in knowing that experience is a language not easily translated, there is a tendency to choose or accept the sameness I start to see everywhere. Sometimes the books and the movies and the songs or whatever else it was on that day would form a chorus like a joke. *God*, I would think in a singsong taunt, *are we really all the same?*

Other times it was more like a prayer. *God? Are we really all the same?*

I love movies not because they're like life but because they aren't. The only thing that is true of movies and life is that they both have to end. I want them most when they are uncanny replicas of life—moments and experiences used like elements rather than reflections. They warp under being watched.

I can rewatch a movie and find my understanding of it totally changed; remembering memories again and again has the effect of making them seem less trustworthy. I have a tendency to see what I like as complete and what I don't like as unfinished, even though I think it should be the reverse. It's the same way that sometimes I talk to a person I once loved and wish I could feel that love for them again. I try to see them under different lights, recall them sitting in different chairs, previous apartments, between subway stops—scenes from a time when I used to notice how they crossed their legs at the knee, or held a pen, before I noticed what I didn't like or couldn't trust. Trying to make them the same as I remember them would require forgetting who they are in the moment. When I tell someone to watch a certain movie I am mostly letting them know something that I am almost ready to say.

Here is *An Unmarried Woman*, which you have to watch; it is my favorite movie. Jill Clayburgh plays Erica, a woman shocked when her husband announces he's fallen in love with a younger woman he met while shopping for shirts. All her anger comes to the surface, and it thrills to see her remove the veneer of the good wife to ask her husband if this new woman is "a good lay," to scream at her new therapist or a bad date, to kick her teen daughter's boyfriend out of their apartment. Even more wonderful are the scenes with her three best friends, in which they show each other what kind of sadness the anger stands in place for.

Here is *Losing Ground*, which you have to watch. It is not really a divorce movie, I guess; more the story of a marriage at the beginning of what could be the end. A marriage on the verge. A professor and her artist husband leave New York City for a summer home, where she can work on her book and he can work on his paintings. They talk to other people more than they talk to each other. They are both easily seduced, still drawn to each other but also to all the hot people they encounter by accident or by fate. "Your husband is a lucky man," the professor's students keep telling her, and she wonders: Why are they so obsessed with my husband? I first saw the film, written and directed by Kathleen Collins, a writer and filmmaker who died too young, at a screening introduced by her daughter. She told us she realized how autobiographical the film had been for her mother as soon as she saw it.

Here is *20th Century Women*, which you have to watch; it is my second-favorite divorce movie that begins with a car on fire. In this movie, it's an accident, but it is also a car previously owned by an ex-husband. Annette Bening, in a voiceover that tells the future and the past at different points of the film, thinks: we brought our baby son home in that car. With an ex-husband who only calls their son, Jamie, on birthdays and holidays, Bening's character, Dorothea, enlists roommates and neighbors to help her raise her son, Jamie, into a man, but her communal-era vision of child-rearing is more rooted in her experience growing up during the Depression than it is in the tail end of the hippie utopian 1970s. "I want to see this modern world," Dorothea says before she makes her roommate Abbie, played by Greta Gerwig, take her to a punk bar. She doesn't like it. Abbie goes too far for Dorothea's taste when she gives Jamie a copy of *Sisterhood Is Powerful*. Reading "The Politics of Orgasm" by Susan Lydon blows his mind; he immediately tells a skateboarding friend that his girlfriend is probably lying about coming if he didn't stimulate her clitoris, and gets his ass kicked for it. At one point Jamie tries to defend, or reassure, his own sense of self. "I'm not all men," he says. "Well, yes and no," his mother says.

Here is *Wild*, which you have to watch; it is my preferred divorced women travelogue movie. I do like the book, but there's something about the movie itself that I feel compelled to return to. I think it has something to do with how visual and present the relationship is between the 1990s and the 1970s, or maybe it's that watching it makes me believe I understand the point of Cheryl Strayed's decision to hike the Pacific Crest Trail, which is an idea so new and strange to my mind that it feels extravagant. Still, I really do think I get it. I get how preparation has nothing to do with avoiding mistakes. How knowledge has nothing to do with experience, but experience has a lot to do with knowledge. How every horizon will always get in the way of what needs to be seen underfoot. How much Strayed needed to bring Adrienne Rich's poems along with her. How there were so many miracles, and so much good luck. How it feels to get something right, simply, after getting something wrong, disastrously.

Here is *Heartburn*, which you have to watch; I like any movie described as "thinly veiled." Nora Ephron's marriage to Carl Bernstein ended after he had an affair while she was pregnant with their second child, and she wrote a "novel" that was adapted into a film Bernstein attempted to sue her for writing. In one report, I remember reading that he alleged the publicity that came with the release of the movie would be damaging to his family; the judge replied that the affair was what had been damaging, and this was only a movie. Anyway, he did get script approval. The movie stars Meryl Streep and Jack Nicholson, and my favorite scene is the one in which Streep, fully dressed and hair pinned up, hides from her own wedding for hours. When her therapist comes in to see what she's so afraid of, Streep tells her marriage is enough. "Marriage doesn't work!" she says. "You know what works? Divorce." "Divorce," the therapist says, as she helps herself to the hors d'oeuvres, "is only a temporary solution."

Ephron is a pivotal architect of the modern romantic comedy, and one of the most notable themes that develop as her work progresses (one that is perhaps only made notable by rewatches in the triple digits) is the way she writes breakups. *When Harry Met Sally*, an ultimate classic of a breakup movie turned romance, is all about Meg Ryan and Billy Crystal learning to let go of their bitterness toward their recent exes and instead love each other, but other movies take a different approach. The heroines of Ephron's most famous and beloved movies commit emotional infidelity, and their boyfriends or fiancés not only forgive them but understand them. In *Sleepless in Seattle*, Meg Ryan's affable fiancé (Bill Pullman, all aw-shucks throughout) is prone to extreme allergies and sweetly nerdy references. His fragile physical state is one of the defining qualities of his character, but it is his emotional fortitude that encourages her to run to Tom Hanks at the top of the Empire State Building. In

You've Got Mail, Meg Ryan's boyfriend is a sweetly pedantic newspaper columnist, played beautifully by Greg Kinnear, his smarm and self-righteousness the perfect foil for Ryan's beloved neighborhood bookstore owner. When she breaks up with him in part because she's having a virtual emotional affair with Tom Hanks, not only does he admit to his own crush on another woman, he takes her out for dinner so they can talk and laugh about the blameless dissolution of their long-term relationship.

This is all a noticeable contrast to *Heartburn*, which as a novel did have a sourness to it. I appreciated the honesty of expressing the bitter heartbreak over the central marriage in the novel, but prefer the lighter touch of the film version. Even still, *Heartburn* is the movie with the real irreconcilable differences, and an ending that's triumphant only because it's allowed the full bittersweetness of a breakup that has no obvious path back to romance. I wonder about the motivation between the fair, dignified, and warm ways Ephron's heroines leave their less worthy placeholder boyfriends: Was it wish fulfillment turned movie magic, the fantasy not of true love but that the lesser loves would fade away without too much pain or anger? Maybe it was a subtle reflection of *The Good Divorce* at work in the movies, with the dream of a more liberal, tolerant world acted out by two characters representing the audience demographics they stood in for.

Anyway, here is *The Brood*, which you have to watch. It is David Cronenberg's horror movie about a husband trying to get custody of his child away from a wife who has joined a viscerally disgusting cult. It has the same sort of ugly rawness of *Kramer vs. Kramer*, with the added bonus of being both emotionally and horror-movie scary: the terror of losing someone to forces beyond your control, plus special effects. I have to admit I prefer it to watching Dustin Hoffman berate Meryl Streep in *Kramer*, though the swoop of Streep's hair at that time of her career remains unmatched.

Here are *The Squid and the Whale*, directed by Noah Baumbach, and *The War of the Roses*, directed by Danny DeVito, both of which you have to watch; they are my mother's favorite movies about divorce. Both movies revolve around the practicalities of divorce—custody battles, real estate divisions—and the way families will fold their feelings into legalese, letting precedents speak so that they don't have to. Both films are satires, in their way, one a gentle and the other a cruelly exaggerated lens on reality, and they both hurt me to look at too closely; they are sometimes so similar to the families my mother and I wrote all those parenting plans for.

When *Marriage Story*, Noah Baumbach's 2019 film about a divorcing couple negotiating custody, was released I watched it with an ear for the language I recognized—two intelligent, sensitive characters, well-versed in the vernacular of therapy and narrative, try their best to say the words that follow the script of a good divorce. In attempting to spare each other's feelings, they accidentally reveal that in the same way they expect to be punished for bad behavior, there might be a reward for behaving well. Anger follows the realization that this is not the case. Examples—car seats, email privacy, school districts—replace the truth when they speak. The best line of dialogue is one of the shortest, during the film's fight scene: a blowup without catharsis. "You wanted me until you didn't," the husband says to his soon-to-be-ex-wife. Is there a better description of how it feels when that happens to you? He says hateful things to her and then weeps on his knees; she touches his hair.

As I watched, I wondered if every woman who ends a marriage

has to comfort her husband through the pain of saying the absolute worst thing he can to a person he wants to hurt as much as he wants to love. Here they've located the pain, but will not admit the reason. The reason it hurts is because they have a different relationship than the one they want. Every other hurt will come from that one; there will be no relief. It's true that if they had been less careful, less kind, less well-versed in the casual legal interventions made on language in the years since no-fault divorce became accessible, they could have hurt each other more. But they never could have hurt each other any less.

For a long time *An Unmarried Woman* was the movie I watched most, and then I stopped, afraid that I would grow sick of it. On one repeat viewing I became irritable watching Erica slowly eat ice cream, annoyed at her habits as though she was a person I had spent too much time with. In reading about the movie—a panacea for wanting to watch without actually watching—I discovered that the woman who played her therapist in the film was an actual therapist, Dr. Penelope Russianoff, who allowed the directors to shoot in her real home where she saw clients. Dr. Russianoff was so hurt by the backlash against her appearance in the film—colleagues thought it unprofessional, prospective clients thought she was playacting—that in 1978 *The New York Times* reported, in an article titled "Film Role Sends Therapist to Therapy," that she had, indeed, returned to her own therapist after a twelve-year hiatus.

Of course, in retrospect it's easy for me to say that her casting, much like the simple and true details about the downtown New York art world, is what gives the movie its power. Maybe if I had seen the movie in its time I'd be less charmed by accuracy. Maybe I'd be more so. I keep watching to decide.

I t took me a long time to find steady work after my husband moved out, and I was always in a state of panic—there never seemed to be a moment when I wasn't thinking about how I could not let it be true that I couldn't support myself, couldn't live without my husband, couldn't pay the rent.

I took jobs sporadically and frantically—brief, strange encounters in which cash was exchanged for work I could do, even if it was not work I fully understood. For a telecommunications company, I interviewed employees who were veterans, and wrote their experiences into stories posted on a job-listings page. One man talked, with great sadness, about how he would never again feel as alive as he did jumping out of a plane, but told me he was basically happy working for a cell phone provider. I wrote product descriptions for a start-up that took generic grocery store items, put them in better packaging, and resold them. I wrote Instagram captions for a chain of gyms, and the website text for a curly haircare brand. I wrote membership surveys for a new chain of coworking spaces. I met the landlord of the building where the first location was being built. He owned lots of buildings in the city, and his daughter was getting married. He wanted to hire a "real" writer to help him with her wedding toast. That's me, I said.

At first I assumed this must be a Cyrano de Bergerac thing—

surely no one would want to admit that they had hired someone to write a wedding toast?—but that was my mistake. A certain kind of rich wants to pay for a certain kind of good. This man intended to tell everyone he had hired a very expensive writer because that's what his daughter was worth. Before me, he had tried to hire a famous singing coach, a woman with some of the most successful pop stars in the world as her clients, and to her credit she listened to him once and then refused to cash his check. She couldn't make him a good singer in time for the wedding, she said. I admired her ethics. That job paid for two months of my rent.

For several weeks I would talk to him on the phone, or sometimes I went to his office. I asked him questions about his daughter and their life together, collected their stories, asked him what other wedding speeches he'd seen and liked. I thought, sometimes, how silly this job was. There was something so sweet about it, talking to this man about his oldest daughter getting married. There was something, too, that felt off. Even more than the transaction itself, I couldn't ignore that his impulse wasn't very pure. He often remarked on how the only thing he really wanted was for this speech to be better than his ex-wife's. I never asked about her and never included anything he offered about her in what I wrote. Instead I wrote and rewrote his stories about taking his daughter to gymnastics competitions, how she had taken care of him after a surgery, how together they loved to watch *The Bachelor* and go to concerts, how proud he was of her education and her work. When the draft was done, I would record myself reading it and send him the voice memos, to give him a sense of how I imagined the cadence, the inflections. In the mornings after I showered I would sit on one of the cheap folding chairs I kept at either end of the cheap table I used as my desk

then, and with my wet hair dripping down my T-shirt I would repeat the speech until my words felt like his.

He didn't invite me to the wedding but wrote after to tell me that
he was thrilled with the response, that everyone had loved it. I
wished I could have gone. I often thought how much the experience
had the feeling of the opening scene to a romantic comedy, and I
would, on the long subway rides home from his office, play out the
plot. If it was a movie, perhaps it would be the kind in which our
heroine loses her job in the middle of an intense, fraught union
drive. She would meet a colleague, a man who represented *everything
she hated* about the industry they worked in. Desperate to pay her
rent, she takes any odd jobs she can get. This leads her to the man
looking to buy a wedding toast, and in the movie version he would
be kind and affable, more in need of help than a service, and he
would invite her to the wedding, where she would meet his oldest
daughter and his three other children: three girls total, and one
boy, who would be revealed to be *the man she hated!* The speech goes
so well that all the other dads in their social circle hire her to keep
writing speeches, and so she is frequently bumping into this same
family at the various weddings they attend.

This boy is the kind of handsome that makes women stupid, the
kind of self-serious and certain that only money can buy. Perhaps
he has a girlfriend with a very prestigious job, something that hits
our heroine where it hurts. But one night they admit that their cute
antagonism is just extended flirting, and maybe they both let their
guard down a little. His father calls—another daughter is getting
married, and he wants her help writing the speech. By now she is
practically a member of the family and gets invited to the rehearsal
dinner, too. There, the family announces that there will be another

wedding soon: their son is engaged to his girlfriend. Our heroine is crushed—devastated—how could he do this to her? The wedding speech she wrote, when the father reads it, is clearly about the son; when the son tries to give his own toast, he has nothing to say. It ends with our heroine standing in the pride of her heartbreak.

As I was writing this movie in my head I told the idea to some friends. This was after I had separated, but I hadn't told them yet. I recounted the story as I saw it in my head, with even more detail. They listened and laughed, and when I was done they asked if this was my way of telling them I was getting divorced. It's *fiction*, I said.

In movies, one can see how the overarching mood of a decade influences the tone of the story. For example, people often tell me they expect me to hate marriage, something I take to be a symptom of a time in which we can tell ourselves there is no reason needed to start or end a marriage, so why would I do so again? I don't hate marriage, but I can see how denying it is a little suspect.

Still, why would the divorced be so inclined to hate marriage? I remind myself: *Not every married person will get divorced, but every divorced person was once married.* Many might go so far as to marry again. "A second marriage," quipped Samuel Johnson, "is the triumph of hope over experience." Even more hopeful than a second marriage to another spouse is remarriage to the original one, like Elizabeth Taylor's to Richard Burton.

The concept of remarriage was always destined to be played as romantic comedy. Its stakes are a little too high to look at closely without some pain, and humor is an excellent medium for lowering them. The best-known "comedies of remarriage," as the philosopher Stanley Cavell called them in his 1981 book, *Pursuits of Happiness,* belong to a small cluster of movies from the Golden Age of Hollywood, an era that saw one of the most profound forms of voluntary censorship with the adoption of the Hays Code as well as the release of incredible movies like *Adam's Rib*, *The Awful Truth*, *His Girl Friday*, and *The Philadelphia Story*.

Convoluted and full of innuendo, overwhelmed with charm and celebrity, the stories took small moments of miscommunication or white lies and stretched them, to great effect, into comedic gold. Journalists took on false identities; socialites swanned over ne'er-do-wells; little sisters meddled and juries deliberated. At the heart of it all was one couple who had called it quits on their marriage, but the audience knew long before the characters did that such separations would only be temporary. In *Adam's Rib*, Spencer Tracy and Katharine Hepburn represent opposite sides in a court case over whether a woman can really be found guilty for attempting to kill her unfaithful husband—a Rorschach test played as a joke. Tracy blusters whenever he witnesses Hepburn's smarts in the courtroom and loses it anytime another man noticeably appreciates her charm. At one point he cruelly, unforgivably pantomimes killing himself in front of her. The movie is about difference—its last words are "Viva la difference!" spoken in and with love—but the core premise is a bitterness familiar to any heterosexual couple who has tried to bluster through the way a woman is judged while a man is understood.

In *The Awful Truth*, Irene Dunne and Cary Grant allow a cascade of white lies—they leave places after they said they'd stay, they see people when they claim to be alone—to undermine their marriage. It's debatable whether either of them is guilty of infidelity, but a real hurt accumulates. If marriage has deadly sins, theirs is pride; if divorce is a fairy-tale punishment, the film must resolve with Dunne and Grant reconciling right before the clock strikes midnight and their divorce is finalized. As the hour approaches, they reflect with the kind of simple dialogue that still hits hardest:

"Things could be the same," Dunne says, "if things were different."
"You're wrong," Grant says, "about things being different because they're not the same. Things are different in a different way."

The plots of these films rest not, in Cavell's words, on how to "get the central pair together, but to get them *back* together, together *again*." Contemporary audiences may recognize their own version of this genre. In the past few decades, there has been a significant revival of movies attempting this same spirit with two current stars: George Clooney and Julia Roberts. In 2001's *Ocean's Eleven*, they played a divorced couple for the first time—their reunion was the heart of the Rat Pack heist remake. Since then, they have played different kinds of long-suffering lovers to each other, often as direct parallels to their celebrity predecessors. The latest addition to the genre is 2022's *Ticket to Paradise*, in which Clooney and Roberts play divorcés bickering over what's best for their grown daughter as she prepares to get married in Bali. This is a movie that manages to conjure the pleasantly opposing textures of gloss and fluff—good shirts, gorgeous landscapes, some mild conflict, and a pretty happy ending—yet maintains a strange distance dispelling those pleasures.

"Something evidently internal to the task of marriage causes trouble in paradise," Cavell writes. "Marriage has its disappointment—call this its impotence to domesticate sexuality without discouraging it, or its stupidity in the face of the riddle of intimacy, which repels where it attracts, or in the face of the puzzle of ecstasy, which is violent while it is tender, as if the leopard should lie down with the lamb." In these disappointments, the grammar of the remarriage genre takes shape. Watch as our heroes and heroines foil their own attempts at the best parts of romance. Watch them interrogate, in slapstick caricature, why one can't just trust commitment to last or desire to sustain itself. See our own uncertainty and fear about the viability of traditional marriage on-screen.

Today, something evidently different about the task of divorce causes trouble in what passes for paradise. At each step toward making divorce legally accessible there have been detractors (if divorce is easy to get, won't more people divorce?) and defenders (if divorce is hard to get, don't people suffer?). Both sides of this debate often assume that changing divorce law will transform society itself. But laws are rarely what create social customs. How people live influences the laws, even as the laws influence how people judge their lives. Ultimately when people are given the right to marry each other they do, and when they have the option to leave each other they do.

The original remarriage movies appeared right after the Depression, when the divorce rate fell and the reasons why were another kind of Rorschach test. The period's low divorce rates could just have easily been the result of the bottlenecking that occurs whenever people are not allowed to shape their lives as they choose. Similarly, after Reagan signed off on the first true no-fault divorce laws in the United States in 1970, fears proliferated that the new laws would rot away any hold that matrimony had on American society. In *Marriage, a History*, Coontz writes about what the media would ten years later call a "divorce revolution." By 1980, one in two marriages were projected to end in divorce. But as with the divorce rates during the Depression, it is hard to say whether more people were formally ending their marriages in the 1970s, or more informally separated people were making things official. An unhappy marriage began to feel like a given. Equitable divorce legislation was made to feel like a privilege.

More striking is the fact that since the middle of the past century, people have become less likely to marry. The so-called divorce revolution wasn't the real threat to marriage; it was the rate of remarriage after divorce. Divorce rates slowed down after 1981, even declining despite the availability of no-fault divorce, but people did not remarry. Two thirds of all American divorced women in the 1950s would marry again within five years of their marriage's dissolution; as the millennium approached, only 50 percent of women were remarried or even cohabitating with another partner five years after their first marriage, even though by 1998 the divorce rate was down 26 percent from 1979. Then again, comparisons aren't exactly helpful—people are marrying less frequently, and therefore divorce appears rare. There are far fewer means for tracking the dissolution of relationships that don't involve a census, a government officiant, an expired lease, or any other similar certificate of proof.

When pundits and politicians stoke a social panic about the end of matrimony, it has less to do with the causes that drive up rates of divorce than with those that drive down rates of remarriage. If people would rather stay single forever—if marriage is neither necessary nor desirable, particularly to women who may also choose not to have children for their own reasons, despite conservative fearmongering and other more subtle forms of social manipulation— then the sanctity of divorce has been lost, too, and the whole institution might be doomed.

Julia Roberts has become the ultimate movie star for embodying this practical and emotional contradiction. Her early career was defined by characters who, like her naive sex worker in *Pretty Woman* and her doomed diabetic young mother in *Steel Magnolias*, were magnetically fun to watch play house. Her own real-life romances were legend and her breakups multiplied, so much so that she starred in two movies parodying this fact about herself (first the warm *Notting Hill*, then the bitter *Runaway Bride*). The generations before her only barely had the same privilege without destroying their box office credibility or ending their careers: actresses had annulments or scandals, but most of all they had a tabloid culture that allowed for only a few carefully guarded secrets. Roberts had, instead, her laughing beauty and an audience who recognized their own choices in hers.

She has already embodied one particularly important type of luxurious divorcée. Twelve years before *Ticket to Paradise*, she starred in the very movie about love and divorce that turned Bali into a setting for spiritual and romantic enlightenment: the film adaptation of *Eat Pray Love*. If anyone could have played Gilbert in the era before no-fault divorce, it would have been Katharine Hepburn, but that wasn't her part to play. After Hepburn divorced her first husband in 1934, she had many famous love affairs—most important, her longtime commitment to Spencer Tracy—though she never did remarry.

Where Roberts is a celebrity who remade the concept in her own image, Clooney is a carefully delineated composite of seemingly every male movie star who came before the social revolution of the 1960s. He represents an era of grand romance, the kind that ends right at the height of a good kiss or the deployment of the right joke. As Daniel Ocean in *Ocean's Eleven*, he paid his debt to the Rat Pack in full, and even in his most contemporary roles there's almost always an easy parallel. His disaffected but righteous army general in *Three Kings* recalls Humphrey Bogart in *Casablanca*; his frantic paranoiac conniving in *Burn After Reading* could be James Stewart in *Vertigo*. He already did an *Adam's Rib* knockoff as part of his ongoing collaboration with the Coen brothers, *Intolerable Cruelty*, a comedy of sour scammers, legal battle, and romance. But he's Cary Grant before he's anyone else: charming, desired, and endlessly exasperating. They both look most comfortable when witnessing someone else's awkwardness. As a movie star, Clooney is meant to be a man who is known for—and loved despite—his limits. "Does he make you laugh?" he asks Roberts in *Ocean's Eleven*, referring to the man she's with instead of him, in an exchange worthy of Grant and Irene Dunne. "He doesn't make me cry," she says. He has no comeback.

Clooney's and Roberts's characters in *Ticket to Paradise* have been divorced for almost twenty years yet have retained the burning animosity of those early breakup days. He's an architect like you see in the movies: wealthy, expertly preserved, and with lots of time on his hands. She's a curator like we've seen in other movies: poised, immaculately dressed, and long-suffering. (I could refer to them by their fictional names, but the entire point of the film is for the audience to enjoy identifying with Clooney's and Roberts's professional personas rather than their assigned roles.) Their daughter is about to graduate from law school and take a much-needed vacation to Bali, presumably from her overly intense parents as much as from the punishing curriculum, with her sweet foil of a roommate. While there, she falls in love with a resident of the island and decides to marry him, walking away from her law school degree to join his family business. It's a very successful business, we're reassured: Clooney is begrudgingly won over when the fiancé tells him that their seaweed product is stocked at Whole Foods.

The size of their new family-by-marriage is emphasized enough times to make the sparseness of Clooney and Roberts's own relations noticeable. Why is it that their daughter has no grandparents, cousins, aunts or uncles, or even more than one friend to invite to the wedding? The grandmotherless cast, according to Cavell, is a convention of the remarriage genre: our movie couples are tethered to neither a past nor a future. Nor are they tethered to concerns about money. "Our films must on the whole take settings of unmistakable wealth," Cavell writes. Only then will "the people in them have the leisure to talk about human happiness, hence the time to deprive themselves of it unnecessarily." Here Roberts and Clooney each try on the role of wealthy boomer parent, with good taste in their things, prideful righteousness in their decisions, and an eclipsing certainty that nothing matters more than their opinion.

As a married couple, we learn, they treated each other more like colleagues than lovers. Now the two of them must, as they've always tried to do, put aside their differences for the good of their daughter—the one thing they can agree on is that they only want the best for her. Their vaguely referenced hopes and dreams for their only child are never really clarified, which suits their unfinished business. Perhaps if they were more than certain of their ideas on their own terms rather than just in opposition to an ex-spouse there would be no reason to keep fighting. Of course, in the hijinks that make up many of the movie's scenes—drunkenness, a snake-bite, emotional betrayal and forgiveness, sliced bananas—they remember that they do make a good team, and that perhaps their strong feelings for each other aren't hate as much as . . . married love. The film ends with them leaping off the boat taking them back to the airport so that they can stay in Bali with their honeymooning daughter; the credits roll alongside a blooper reel, so that we know how much fun everyone had making it.

I found myself berating *Ticket to Paradise* for falling short of the old remarriage comedies—the charm, wisdom, and refreshing cynicism with which they handled the tense yet sexy dynamics of a couple trying not to want each other. Then I berated myself for expecting too much. Is it expecting too much to want a movie to be as good as its inspiration, or at least to expect it not to embody such a political regression?

With few exceptions, the earlier remarriage movies included no children, a detail from which Cavell infers the main characters' sublimated desire to be kids again, or at least allow themselves the easy immaturity of innocence. Clooney and Roberts do take a vacation from themselves in *Ticket to Paradise*, loosening up as they learn to harvest seaweed and make small talk with their new in-laws. But now they also need their unjaded daughter to teach them about love. Their generation was burned by their attempts, but hers still has the chance to believe that they could make it all better. The film helps clarify why childlessness is a convention of so many remarriage films: children in movies have an unfortunate habit of acting as moral compasses that point toward the most conservative option. When Clooney cynically tells his would-be son-in-law that nothing lasts forever, the young man warmly but self-righteously responds that marriage is supposed to. When Roberts tells her daughter she doesn't know what she's getting into, her daughter correctly tells Roberts that she's only speaking to her younger, dumber self. Perhaps that's the other function of romantic comedies, to pleasantly acknowledge how our present hurt disorients our sense of possibility.

The women who starred in these original remarriage comedies, Cavell observed, belonged to the same generation. Claudette Colbert, Irene Dunne, Katharine Hepburn, Rosalind Russell, and Barbara Stanwyck were all born between 1898 and 1907 and were in their late twenties or early thirties at the height of the genre. They were sardonic without cynicism, cutting without bitterness. They had seen enough of life and men to know better but not so much they knew it all. These actresses had been raised by suffragettes, white women who, as Cavell puts it, "won the right to vote without at the same time winning the issues in terms of which voting mattered enough." They inherited the right to "not settle," and in this basic tenet of almost-freedom grew a threat: if they wouldn't settle at all, then someone else—frighteningly, maybe a husband—must accept less than what they believed was their due.

But not settling poses problems for narrative. What defines the opposite of settling, and who gets to say when it has been accomplished? "This in effect interprets the idea of a love potion—of whatever the thing is that makes love possible," said Cavell, "or recognizable—as providing the gift of pastlessness, allowing one to begin again, free of obligation and of the memory of compromise."

The remarriage plot strives to bring balance where none can exist. Alternatives to marriage and monogamy may exist, and to prove it, here is a parade of glamorous, respected, talented, and intelligent divorcées, who have all had their freedom—for a moment—and who, we'll see, will choose marriage again now that they are ready for happiness. Call it the ratification of "cruel optimism," Lauren Berlant's theory of choosing what hurts with the belief that it could still prove, despite all evidence to the contrary, a ticket to paradise.

There's a quotation from another one of Berlant's books, *The*

Female Complaint, that I return to often, about the melodramas of the 1940s and 1950s. This was another defining genre born out of a time when movies wouldn't or couldn't say certain things, and rather than protect viewers from the immorality the Hays Code supposedly feared, it created a new visual language for romance right alongside a still-developing social language for love and family. Many of these films were made by artists and performed by actors who had every reason to doubt their messages: happy endings or bittersweet reunions written by those who had lost their entire families in the Holocaust, straight marriages depicted by closeted people, stories of racism overcome through hard work produced by privileged white people.

But these movies weren't just selling false hope. This worked in the opposite way, too. Stories about broken hearts that killed were told by lovers who had survived. Unbearable yearnings for what wasn't possible were shown by the people who never stopped fighting for more than they thought they could get. Suffragettes, civil rights activists, organizers—many of them took second careers in which they could become the architects of what is, depending on your perspective, either cynical or fantastical movie magic. "All of these women were frank about their politics and their sentimentality," says Berlant. "They were all critics and sustainers of fantasy as a mode of disappointment management or adaptation and of interruption of the realism of the present. They wrote fictions as well as journalism, produced analyses of fantasy in its relation to the lived real."

An easy mistake would be to watch these films or read these books and decide that what lies on the surface is matched by the artist's intention. We can't know what goes on in anyone else's head, but we can give credit where credit is due—we can offer a reading that is marked by the same combination of cynicism and romanticism that exists within us, not quite so contradictory as their official definitions might have us believe. Cynicism needs romance the same way marriage needs divorce. Both are choices that we make, even when they feel like the inevitable dusk that falls as the sun sets.

In all the conversations in which I find myself asked to explain or defend a position about divorce, there seems to be an unspoken assumption that divorce makes the difference between a trap and freedom. Marriage contains. Divorce, then, must be a release. An unhappy marriage can without question become a cage, and the euphoria one feels after leaving a bad relationship can be a liberating rush. But if not marriage, or at least long-term committed monogamy, what else? A story's inquiry into what went wrong with a divorcing couple can be fitted to almost any genre. If not in tears, why not a smile? Cavell wrote that it is "as though you know you are married when you come to see that you cannot divorce, that is, when you find that your lives simply will not disentangle. If your love is lucky, this knowledge will be greeted with laughter." Leave newlyweds and the never-married to their own devices, these films suggest. Divorce is where real romance resides.

During the brief period that I have been someone capable of overidentifying with a story about divorce, I haven't just reserved my thinking for provocation in conversations. I've wondered about it privately and with an appreciation for the contradictions one is afforded when one keeps their mouth shut. (When writing about comparing one's own life to the movies, Cavell said the "moral of this practice" was "to educate your experience sufficiently so that it is worthy of trust. . . . I think of this authority as the right to take an interest in your own experience.")

Alone in the dark there is the impulse to see continuities that prove our favorite theories. Roberts and Clooney are eager to stand inside a film history that moves in a straight line, the concessions to updated divorce laws and customs a plot inconvenience easily dispatched. Most of the answers remarriage movies offer are from the same questions of the original genre. So women can have their own work; they still need love, don't they? So men can relinquish control over the family unit; they're still fun to have around, aren't they?

But then, another continuity between the remarriage movies appears: a fade to black of that time when the divorced couple was actually divorced. *The Philadelphia Story* opens with Grant and Hepburn in an exaggerated pantomime of him moving out, and then cuts to two years later, when her second wedding date is just days away. *His Girl Friday* only has the characters referencing their former marriage, but never shows it. *The Awful Truth* and *Adam's Rib* use the threat of an upcoming separation as a crisis to be averted, never lived through. In *Ticket to Paradise* the only hints we get of their divorced life are brief scenes of Clooney and Roberts at their respective workplaces, constantly interrupting their own lives to revisit and rekindle their animosity. Like the narrowing scope as newlyweds drive off into the distance, their honeymoon and eventual domesticity only gestured to, a character's divorced life is better left to the imagination.

What of the *Eat Pray Love* genre? I get to ask myself then. What of the Elizabeth Gilberts of the world, or *Under the Tuscan Sun* and *It's Complicated*? What of the heroines I love from the 1970s and beyond, Jill Clayburgh's performance in *An Unmarried Woman* and Collins's real clothes worn in *Losing Ground* and Ephron's key lime pie in *Heartburn?* Are they deviations that show the promised alternatives to monogamy and marriage, or are they, in their sometimes complex yet almost always resolute endings, continuations of the same options? Cavell thought the women of the films he chose subjected themselves to this blurry view of their own past and frequent lectures from their ex-husbands about their options for the future because "they know they need to learn something further about themselves, or rather to undergo some change, or creation, even if no one knows how the knowledge and change are to arrive"—something still true of even the most radical attempts to show a romance beyond what the genre has already permitted.

Well, movies are movies, and life is life. They could be the same if they weren't different, but the movies could never not be fiction. "When it started it was unreal," Clooney says at one point in *Ticket to Paradise.* "And then," he sadly continues in the voice of someone waiting to be proven wrong, "it got real."

ecause I don't tell stories, everyone thinks I have secrets. I try, I swear I try, but I end up making eye contact with the table and saying non sequiturs so nonsensical I might as well be speaking in tongues. As a result, my friends and I are alike in that none of us had any idea why my marriage ended. (We are different in that they think they can find the answer, and I know I never will.) *I'm thinking*, I protest when my friends tell me I'm too quiet, but I do have a secret, and it's that I have a broken television set where my brain used to be. I am ashamed of the lo-fi quality of my thoughts. They are constant and circular, a staticky skimming of the surface.

One afternoon I made a friend admit she thought I was secretive, because I wanted to fight her. "You never even tweeted about your divorce," she said as an explanation. "I don't think not tweeting is the same as keeping a secret," I said, and she shrugged.

The only person we can reliably keep a secret from is ourselves. Almost all others come with exceptions. Like how we accept that anything we tell our friends they'll tell their significant others. (*I'm only telling you this*, a friend I loved once said to me before they told me someone else's secret, *because they're a liar*.)

I came closest to expressing real anger when a new friend told me she assumed I didn't think about my divorce that much because I barely talked about it. I considered my response, waiting for my heart rate to level before I spoke. Each word came out with a tell-tale beat: "It would be a mistake," I said, "to consider talking the best indicator of thinking."

Later, when I was calmer, I thought again. Once I had thought of nothing else but my marriage and my husband. To think less at all felt like a lapse I couldn't let myself admit to; to speak at the same volume as my thoughts might reveal more than I could risk.

I took the subway to visit a friend one day. I arrived exactly when I said I would. (Being punctual is like being superstitious, if you think about it. It means you believe that time exists.) I stayed until evening. My friend lit candles when the sun went down. I sat at the head of their long wooden table while her husband lay on their overstuffed couch, pretending to read—trying to seem like he wasn't eavesdropping, but every so often he would twist his head around the arm of the couch to face me and ask a question about what I'd just said. I did my best to answer him as he asked what happened when, which event followed the introduction of which new man, which moment came after which ending.

At a certain point he sat up on his elbows and began to speak plainly but beautifully about their marriage. He told me, very simply, that he had never thought he would be a man who could be strange about understanding his wife in relation to himself. He had maybe never thought of himself as a man who would feel anything other than the most straightforward expression of his good feelings. He would always be able to see her for how she existed in the world, almost like how he saw her hair color, a favorite outfit, a deftness for parallel parking or mixing a certain drink—something he would enjoy for the happiness it brought her, but that had nothing to do with him. An example of what had made him fall in love with her.

Now, he told me, he realized how stupid that had been. He saw that he had not been thinking about how he would be a husband, or what that role might do or demand of him. He had needed to ignore the way he felt about his own work, and had been unprepared to find himself in some classic, awful clichés: the man with a pretty good career who was still jealous of his wife's success, for example. The husband learned late that competition and desire want each other very badly. That they are perhaps almost alike.

I waited for him to say more. I like when husbands talk to me about their marriages. He waited, too. I realized he was pausing because he was implying something about the story he had heard me tell.

"I know what you're thinking," I started, his face patient and still half resting on the pillow. "And I appreciate it, I really do. But you're wrong. That's not what happened. That's not why our marriage ended."

"Are you sure?" he asked.

"Yes," I said. "Very sure."

Weeks later I would be in the shower and this conversation would come back to me, hot and bright behind my eyes. I spat water at my feet. *Oh my god*, I thought. I wasn't sure at all.

Could it really be that simple? My uncertainty made me more susceptible to other people's certainties; even resisting such straightforward descriptions seemed, in itself, a cliché. Of course I would deny any reason offered; of course I would deny any reason at all, I imagined people thinking as I explained why they were right about almost everything, just wrong about what had happened to me.

Later (too late) I would learn that the people most certain that they knew how other people should live were those least certain of their own lives. Their convictions were often seductive or charming. Still, not all of them were wrong, and some of them were doing exactly what I had sought out in narratives first and therapy second: like my friend's husband listening from the couch, their perspective was their generosity and my defensiveness just that, a wall put up to avoid seeing what they saw so clearly. Of course I thought of my marriage as something beyond understanding, my divorce too unique to fit into any other story. I knew it was true that something between my ex-husband and me had shifted when I got a job more like the one he had; it was true much of the identity of our relationship rested on us both believing that he took care of me, in many different material ways; it was true that by the time we left each other I had begun to wonder if changing so much of my life had changed the way we saw each other. "I don't want to be with you because I need you," I told him often in our last year of living together, "I want to be with you because I want you." I was trying to reassure us both. I was admitting more than I knew.

I n 1970, the filmmaker Arthur Ginsberg owned one of the first Sony Portapaks in the United States: a one-person battery-operated, self-contained videotape recording system. He wanted to use it for a behind-the-scenes documentary about the making of a pornographic film. Carel Rowe and Ferd Eggan were amateur filmmakers looking to film their wedding night and sell it to repay some debts. Ginsberg agreed. Five years later, the three of them ended up with something else entirely: thirty hours of sporadically filmed footage, an excruciating document of their brief engagement, staged—but legally binding—wedding, short marriage, and eventual breakup.

Self-described as "two freaky people going straight," their decision to marry is a mystery. "Why go all the way?" Ginsberg asks them at one point. Rather than answer, they monologue. They want what they want because they want it, and they find many different ways to say that. A predecessor of reality television, it's an exercise in endurance. How long will it take for them to stop pretending they don't notice the camera and instead start letting the camera take what it needs? How long can the audience stand the repetition, the posturing, the performance, and what will be the payoff?

The Continuing Story of Carel and Ferd was meant to be watched as a three-channel, eight-monitor video installation accompanied by a live camera feed of the audience as they watched it. Carel Rowe and Ferd Eggan were intended to be present. It was first shown in this more artistic format at the New York performance space the Kitchen in 1971. In the carpeted room of Electronic Arts Intermix, a nonprofit video archive based in SoHo, New York, I watched a one-hour version repackaged for WNET's 1975 series *Video and Television Review*. The genre gets confused, as what was an art film is now a lo-fi documentary remixed for a television and not a gallery audience; the film begins with the fast-moving and slowly pixelating logos of public access television networks. The credits end to reveal Ginsberg sitting with Carel, Ferd, and the show's host, discussing the footage in the round. They are smoking, legs crossed as they recline low in their seats. They all have that VHS aura: a halo radiating against the blue backdrop of the studio.

The Continuing Story of Carel and Ferd is a collection of scenes edited lightly, or not at all. Conversations circle without conclusion. At certain points, the scenes will cut back to the studio interview, where, five years removed from what we just watched, Carel and Ferd comment with updates or epiphanies. There are, occasionally, descriptive texts printed on the bottom of the screen, like LATER THAT DAY and THE WEDDING and EVANSTON ILLINOIS 1971. They admit to self-editing—to making some decisions as to how they would appear on tape, presenting aspects of themselves they thought would be more acceptable or entertaining. Carel wears a turtleneck with a knotted scarf in one scene, a long chain necklace with a heavy pendant. "Stop directing me!" she says. "This is real life."

Carel speaks in song lyrics: laconic metaphors, crisp signifiers. Every sentence sounds like she should be winking at the end of it, which she sometimes does. This is because she was, in her first marriage, catapulted into being a songwriter. About ten years before shooting *The Continuing Story*, she was a cheerleader at the University of Arizona in Tucson, enough in love with a folk singer named Travis Edmonson to follow him to San Francisco, though not in enough of a relationship with him to have his phone number when she arrived.

Carel hunted down the manager of the Kingston Trio, Frank Werber, thinking that maybe he would know how to contact Edmonson. Instead, Werber sent her three dozen roses and by the end of her summer vacation had asked her parents for her hand in marriage. Carel described it as going from cheerleader to trophy wife. On their first date, Werber introduced her to the jazz musician Vince Guaraldi, who played her the instrumental classic "Cast Your Fate to the Wind." "It was like a scene in *Casablanca*," Carel reminisced in a 2012 radio interview. "Frank sauntered into the club, introduced me to Vince, and said, 'Okay, Vince, play it for her.'" Vince told Carel he wanted lyrics, which she wrote driving back and forth over the Golden Gate Bridge and thinking about Travis Edmonson. The lyrics to the last verse of "Cast Your Fate to the Wind" are:

So now you're old, you're wise, you're smart
You're just a man with half a heart

With the royalties from that song Carel refashioned herself into a filmmaker. When she introduces herself to Ginsberg's camera, she says she makes documentaries and shorts, describing them as "beautiful films." She taught film school for two years, did commercials, but couldn't get work. "Being a girl, I couldn't get into the American Film Institute . . . because every time I get a job as a camerawoman I was taking away someone else's job. They had families, I was a career woman." When she finishes that story she winks.

Before beginning production on what would become *The Continuing Story of Carel and Ferd*, Carel had worked on about twenty "fuck films," as she calls them, estimating that she had acted in about thirteen and done editing, sound, or directing for the others. "Making fuck films ruined my life completely," Carel says. "It's not as though if I made food commercials that I wouldn't eat. But fucking is all in your head, and when they turn the lights on and it's not in your head, you just have to reach back in there and commit the sin of fantasy." She thinks for a moment. "I wish I could think of a metaphor but I'm dropping off again."

Carel divorced Frank. Ferd was, at the time of the filming, an openly bisexual man struggling with a heroin addiction. When they describe their postmarital plans, Ferd talks in junkie logic. He is kicking dope, of course, and he'll do it by going back to live with his parents for a month. There's no dope there, he explains, and he wouldn't take any with him because he couldn't afford it even if he wanted to, not that he does.

The details of how they met are glossed over, which adds to the feeling of starting a story in the middle. Carel made a film with Ferd, part of their ongoing attempt to write pornography as a coherent narrative. As Ferd describes it, not only was the film "hated by everyone who saw it, audiences left notes saying it was ugly and had nothing to do with love." It was an S&M movie; Ferd somewhat pointedly says they made it because Carel was "under the impression she was into" it. Carel does not dispute this. "Yeah," she responds, no longer rating fantasy as a sin, "movies are real thera-peutic, you can just act out your fantasies in a script." She does take offense to his description of it as a horrible movie, saying if they were in sync it would have been a good movie. "We're hardly pro-fessional," she quips to the camera, the wink back in her voice. "But we mean well."

At the time, Ferd was dating Gary Indiana, who appears only once, but his status as Ferd's lover results in one of the film's true fight scenes. If Ferd really does get married and return to Illinois, Gary says to Ferd but for the camera, he'll take strychnine and then lie in a coffin like Sarah Bernhardt with a dozen American Beauty roses draped across his chest.

In 1999, Indiana wrote a profile on Ferd for *POZ* magazine. We should all be so lucky to have our former lovers describe us the way Indiana does. Physically, he says Ferd was "a rakish Nordic syba-rite: a queerly angled face with concupiscence (a word he'd defi-nitely use) written all over it, a suggestion of world-weary anguish in his hooded eyes." Emotionally, Indiana says that "in the nether-world we lived in then, Ferd was a thinking person's love god, sur-rounded by many boyfriends and a female fiancée, a dandy whose air of languid, charismatic decadence spoke to a general disen-chantment, after Manson and Altamont, with the concept of 'good vibrations.'"

Ginsberg is less lucky to have Indiana's attention. He describes the film as "a vague project that soon became an endless documentary." While that endless documentary was evolving, Indiana explains, he flew home to Boston and had "a nice long nervous breakdown, the onset of which you can see in the video." In his one scene he takes Carel's cigarette and uses it to light his own, the uneasy affinity that naturally occurs between two people fucking the same man on display. It reminded me how much I miss smoking, which is to say, it reminded me how much I miss having an excuse to share something with someone that feels good enough to ignore how bad it is for both of us.

Other characters include Richard, who Ferd calls an "old friend" of Carel's in a tone of voice that makes it clear what kind of relationship it actually is. Carel describes him as a "wealthy older man," draping the word *wealthy* in a manner that recalls how Richard wears his scarf. Richard, credited without a last name but later referred to in Indiana's memoirs as a Paramount executive, does not like this marriage; Richard does not like this film. Richard likes Carel and Carel's films, but he does not understand, and he does not approve of whatever this is. "It's going to be a huge downer for everyone watching. To watch someone getting married? Marriage is a wet blanket on a relationship. I mean . . . marriage doesn't *last* in America! It just doesn't last!" He does not get why, if they want to make a movie about the consummation of a wedding night, they actually have to consummate a wedding. "Make the commitment! Just don't sign any papers!"

"Marriage can transcend the legality," Ferd retorts. "We want to go through the hassle. We want to tie the knot." Richard remains unconvinced. Richard knows they want to tangle the knot.

Before the wedding Carel and Ferd fight about Indiana. "Gary was lying in my lap, and I was holding him, and Carel got real pissed off," is how Ferd describes the night before. Carel says Ferd is always *languishing* with other men—her enunciation carries the meaning she's not yet willing to put into words. Ferd's response is: What other men have I ever *languished* with? During this fight Ferd

posits that she might be nervous, and she might be trying to say theatrical things for the camera. "I don't want to gain new lovers!"
Carel says. "I don't want a continual stream of excess people inter-
fering and directing and meddling with and . . . acting as catalysts.
I don't want all those outside forces of lovers, those intense little
lover things, all these other people."

On their wedding day, someone remarks that for the first time
they seem speechless. "We're struck dumb with terror and awe,"
says Ferd. He got a haircut and is wearing a suit. Carel wears a tur-
ban and big earrings. They're both beautiful. Guests are taking
photos of the camera instead of the couple. The wedding vows are
about marriage as a media show: "The rings you are about to exchange will bind your marriage by sight, the media will bind it by
the minds, and you will soon consummate it in action. That this
marriage will not be complete until its separation from the media
disappears." There are Hebrew blessings for the wine, and Ferd
stamps on the glass.

In the scene where they attempt to consummate the marriage,
they move slowly and with far less energy than they had for each
other in earlier scenes. (They admit later this did not technically
happen on tape; we see the beginning, but no finale.) "That was the
first time I had the feeling that the video thing—not the movie so
much—but the fact of the video was there, and all these other people were standing around watching . . . it was for everybody else,"
Ferd reflects. "We hadn't gotten married. The television audience
had just had a marriage." Carel calls it an orgy marriage. Ferd
continues that he felt like they were the only people involved in the
production who thought it was real. "It was encrusted with all this
media hardware, but it was still a real experience. We were really

getting married." I believe him. Performance is not without sincerity.

Later, Ferd will say in the studio that he cannot figure out what this documentary is, saying it is "obviously not entertainment. It's not soap opera. It's too real." "Oh, I disagree," says Carel. "I think it's titillation and entertainment from a soap opera point of view. That's the sick love story of it, that's what they get out of it." As with most arguments between formerly married people, they're both right, but I would never tell them that. ("This is a McLuhan nightmare," Carel comments later from the studio set.)

The second half of the film is too lonely to look at, too intimate to look away from. I would have watched all thirty hours if they had been available, and also I hoped it would end every minute it played. Like a marriage, the film is the story of two people who have what they are not even sure they want. Like a marriage, the film only feels like it could last forever. Carel and Ferd have moved to Illinois, where she gets a job at a bakery for $1.59 an hour, and Ferd reports that he is sober. This is when Ferd and Carel were left alone with the camera. Apparently Ginsberg could no longer be in the room with them. The feeling was mutual. In one scene Carel calls Ginsberg "awful Arthur" when she sees him after a few months apart, laughing as she says she's trying to get away from "the video vampires." Instead they interview each other: Ferd wants to know if she acts childish on purpose, so that she will be treated like a child. Carel wants Ferd to know she doesn't really believe he's gay. "Well, I assure you I am," he says.

In 1973, *An American Family* premiered on PBS. Edited into twelve episodes from three hundred hours of footage shot over seven months, the original airing had a weekly average of ten million viewers and is considered the first true reality television show. Margaret Mead said *An American Family* was "as new and significant as the invention of drama or the novel," while Jean Baudrillard said the show was a sign of "dissolution of TV in life, dissolution of life in TV." It was supposed to be a documentary about the Louds (I swear that is their real name), an average upper-middle-class family living in California.

Coincidentally or not—there is some question as to whether the producers manipulated the family for more drama—it ended up being a document of the parents' separation and eventual divorce. Fiction wasn't immune to similar scrutiny about its responsibility to truth or moral compass. That same year, Ingmar Bergman released his miniseries, *Scenes from a Marriage*, the brutally drawn-out six-episode story of how a marriage turns into a divorce. Its excruciating realness in depicting how a husband and wife are unable to really get away from the fact of their former relationship, able to live neither with nor without the other, contributed to a small moral panic that audiences would be inspired to get divorced themselves.

From the 1970s to the 1990s, the providence of reality television stayed similar, angling to get behind closed doors. This was, I think, a response to the increasingly hermetic nature of the domestic unit. As families became smaller and more self-contained—less a part of their communities—what happened in these tiny enclaves became a matter of intense interest, the impolite questions the ones we most need answers to. The illicit imaginings of what a neighbor might be doing or saying, paired with the accountability a camera provides, makes the boredom of reality worth it. With the advent of competition-based reality shows in the early 2000s, the scope changed drastically, particularly as streaming services began to produce their own versions of network staples like *The Bachelor* and *Love Island*; Netflix, capitalizing on the early-aughts nostalgia of the Christian fantasy that was Nick Lachey and Jessica Simpson's MTV series *Newlyweds*, made Lachey and his second wife, Vanessa, the face of their own specific brand of high-stakes, claustrophobic reality-romance programming. They could conceivably be called dating shows, though if you have not watched for yourself, they are more accurately understood by their tone: imagine if a heterosexual marriage was edited and scored to match the tenor of a death-defying athlete undertaking the scariest risk of their career, and you will get close to the feeling *Love Is Blind* and *The Ultimatum* conjure in their episodes.

Ferd and Carel's film, released in 1975, two years after *An American Family*, does not exactly fit into the historical arc of reality programming, but it shares the same moods—the desire to be watched taking shape around the shame of vanity, of need. Ferd and Carel call this the Carson Complex, the idea that somewhere inside everyone is the sense that they should be thinking of their life as a stoically comedic anecdote they'll share when a late-night host inevitably calls for an interview. Carel says she doesn't consider it a complex because Johnny Carson is "fantastic." Instead, it's the pressure to be really good on tape—"self-effacing," she clarifies. "The camera gives you a choice of realities, doesn't it?"

Ferd and Carel both had their own celebrity ambitions, and they share that they used to debate if it would be better to be rich or famous. Ferd says he married Carel thinking that they were all in an "Andy Warhol movie—closer to *Trash* than *Empire*. It turns out you can't be in a movie all the time." "Now," Carel says, "all I want is to be employed." Ferd echoes her. "Given that it's 1975 and the country is falling apart, I just want to be employed."

Ferd died in 2007, his obituary describing him as "a veteran of the 'new left'" and crediting him as the cowriter and coproducer of *The Continuing Story of Carel and Ferd*. He hosted the launch meeting for DAGMAR (Dykes and Gay Men against Racism/Repression/ the Right Wing/Reagan), the first activist group structured around HIV/AIDS advocacy in Chicago, and the demonstrations they participated in contributed to, among other successes, the opening of the AIDS ward at Cook County Hospital. From 1993 to 2001 he was the AIDS coordinator for the City of Los Angeles, and fought for safe housing, needle exchanges, and initiatives for women living with AIDS. He once said a beautiful thing about his own organizing that I paraphrase all the time, because so many moments call for it: once you realize you can't do everything, he said, you're free to do anything.

I often return to Indiana and his love letters. Ferd appears as a central character in Indiana's 2015 memoir, *I Can Give You Anything But Love*. He told *The White Review* that he had known it was an important friendship for him, but that writing the book released him

from "certain myths" he had told himself about their relationship—
primarily that Ferd always felt that he was doing what he should be
doing, and Indiana always felt like that was true of Ferd, but not at
all true about himself. Ferd was a writer and artist who wanted
more time to do that work; Indiana admits to a feeling of guilt for
not becoming more politically active. He says he can't imagine that
Ferd's other friends would find his portrait of him at all adequate,
but then, most of us prefer our own lens for the people we love. He
writes more of the triangle that existed between himself, Ferd, and
Carel (their shared cigarette), saying he thought of himself as a
"wayward urchin they'd irresponsibly adopted," part of their collection of people. He reminisced about the pull he felt toward Carel
as well as Ferd, how spellbinding she was: She had the "vibe of
somebody who'd lived the nightmare in a big, expensive way . . .
she seemed implacable enough to launch a military coup in South
America."

Watching *The Continuing Story of Carel and Ferd*, I was so drawn to
their cavalier way of being: their certainty that they could make
marriage into a bit, their crumbling in the face of marriage made
real. But I also saw their cruelty toward each other. Carel was unwilling to accept Ferd for who he was, and Ferd resentful that Carel
made him responsible for the conditions of their marriage. Though
maybe I'm wrong. No one knows what goes on in a marriage except the people in it, the truism goes. I have often thought that the
sentence could stand to be shortened to *No one knows what goes on in a
marriage.*

My friends and I share a fixation on frequencies: the belief that everyone is tuned in to something we can't hear or knows something they aren't saying. We believe ourselves to be alone in silence, while a better ear could hear the hum. I think again of secrets: how keeping them is maybe a measure of safety, another way to stop someone else from knowing first what we've yet to decide about our own lives. "My marriage will be different," my friends say, and I agree not because they are right but because I have already been proven wrong. In truth, I don't know how different any marriage is from another. I think some couples choose to think they are building a marriage, and others choose to believe they are moving into a marriage, but either way they need it to be a shelter. "Who is to say whether a love relation is real or really something else, a passing fancy or trick someone plays (on herself, on another) in order to sustain a fantasy?" wrote Lauren Berlant in *Desire/Love*. "This is a psychological question about the reliability of emotional knowledge, but it is also a political question about the ways norms produce attachments to living through certain fantasies. What does it mean about love that its expressions tend to be so *conventional*, so bound up in institutions like marriage and family, property relations, and stock phrases and plots?" Anyway, my friends and I share a preoccupation with endings.

Though we often remark on how many of our parents are divorced, nobody knows how to break up. We are not willing to accept that sometimes the best way to love is to leave.

Friends should have known better before asking my opinion on anything, that first year of living without my husband. Mostly they wanted to talk about their marriages. Lots of people were in long-term, committed relationships; most of those were couples who lived together. Many of them had multiple sexual or romantic relationships and a single committed partner. Many more talked, at length, about whether they should do the same. Some of them wanted to get married. Some of them didn't. The ones who did end up marrying and the ones who didn't were mostly what I expected, in that I knew I could have never guessed the result. All of them asked for my opinion. Life is so long, I thought while I listened, and marriage is so short.

My divorce happened when I was relatively young. Afterward came a sequence of time when I often felt like I was moving between the phases of other people's lives. I concentrated very hard when my friends and I talked, trying to think of the way I was as the way I had been: as though I was no longer the kind of person who kept measuring, in her head, the millimeters of distance I had put between myself and the person I once believed would put everything into place. Many of my friends had already had formative, life-changing breakups. Many more were making serious commitments to their current partners. Some were older and talking about second marriages. Some were younger and about to live with a person they loved for the first time. The more I heard other people's stories, the more certain I became that every person is the same, and that every person is the only one of their species. When I could pretend to have the detached eye—a sought-after opinion—I would notice that even when we were experiencing completely different phases we spoke about them in the same way. When we were in love, we needed to describe. When we were heartbroken, we needed to explain. We were always trying to convince ourselves.

I wasn't as blunt with my friends as I had been with my mother. I never told anyone to leave their spouse, and I never told anyone not to get married. I knew that those were opinions nobody needed. Marriage requires a couple to get a license, while divorce gives you one: permission to feel bad, behave badly, to experience a peculiar sensation of relief and dread as though they are the same emotion. Here is freedom. Next, surely, is disaster.

It is not that marriage is unknowable, but that we seem to get close to it and it's so completely what we should have expected that it is unfaceable. When someone manages an ending, even abruptly or badly, we pry—we want to know why, we want to know how, and we want to know now. Even if I didn't say the words, I let people know how I felt; when asked, I told them what I thought. One night a friend pulled me aside as we walked between parties, the rest of our friends ahead of us, to say her boyfriend of many years wanted to marry her and she was unsure. "But we've lived together for so long," she explained, trying to rationalize her own fear. "What difference will marriage make, really?" "It'll make a difference," I said, giving her my pain as though it was just a shrug, tossing off my failures like they would be hers. "I didn't think getting married would change anything, either," I reminded her. "I thought my marriage would be the same as living together. But it did, it *did*, it did change," I said, and in memory it is as if I were unable to stop talking once I started. "So what happened?" she countered when she could, as curious as any scalpel. "What changed?"

In the summer of my first year living without my husband, I asked everyone to tell me the story of their life. We were in the right season for gossip—confidences rise and fall with the heat index. When the sun was high we talked about who we had crushes on and who we hated. When the sun went down and we had the decency of shade we asked for more. I was not so concerned with honesty. "True story" is already something of an oxymoron. And I have learned, the way all gullible people must, that the people who proudly declare they have the best stories are usually just liars. The people who really do have the best stories never introduce themselves that way. They wait to be asked. In any case, I just wanted to know how they would lead me through a story that ended the moment they chose the chair in front of mine. The good gossips among them knew how to deflect—"Tell *me* the story of *your* life," they'd say—but no matter who went first we always started, or claimed to start, at the beginning.

There are many fictions to write about one's marriage, and even more about one's family. Divorce encourages a narrative, but not quite the same kind. Here the facts are paramount, the timeline etched as history. *Tell me your love story*, I like to ask couples who have one when we're sitting across from each other with wineglasses and white tablecloths between us, as I rest my chin in my hand with my elbow on the table next to the remains of our dinner and let them reminisce. I don't ask the same question about a divorce story unless the wine has given me the delusion that I have a mental acuity that approximates a pad of yellow legal paper, a pencil, glasses on the bridge of my nose, and a transcript to refer to for accuracy. We give our trust to newlyweds as a gift, but with divorcés it's different. We suspend our disbelief for romance and romance only. With divorcés, if they're lucky, they get our compassion without condescension.

Though now that I'm thinking about it, maybe we give the newly wed and the newly separated the same level of compassionate condescension. *Aww*, we say, *good for you*. Something rosy about that time, which I guess is a function of novelty, feels like it is worth protecting.

I began asking people to tell me their love story after reading the book *Parallel Lives: Five Victorian Marriages* by Phyllis Rose. It was published to critical acclaim in 1983—the second of several books by the critic and professor. The book is a group biography of several notable Victorians and their marriages, chronicling the ways in which people without easy access to divorce got very creative (which is to say, very weird) in negotiating their breakups and makeups. The author did not choose writers because they are necessarily more inventive in living—far from it—but because they tend to be diligent reporters of their lives, leaving us more material to work with. Rose selected many kinds of marriages: ones that were enshrined either by law or by choice, sexual or sexless, with children or without. She also included subjects with many kinds of politics, ranging from liberal to what she calls "romantic authoritarians," their homes the stage to act out their relationship to power.

Marriage, Rose believes, is the primary political experience of adulthood, as intimate a contract with your partner as it is with the state that issues the license. Every society arranges strictures around the family, and often it's by looking at individual relationships that we see how and where those strictures failed and what might replace them. A how-to is an overvalued directive. What I want is a how-did: How *did* they live? "We are desperate for information about how other people live because we want to know how to live ourselves," Rose writes, "yet we are taught to see this desire as an illegitimate form of prying."

The Victorians may have made their codes more explicit, but contemporary times are not freer; they are only subtler. Today, when marriage holds so many outsize hopes and lowered expectations, we are no surer of what the institution means or what role it should play. *Parallel Lives* shows how these stories were used to start political and moral inquiries into marriage itself.

The couples in the book—Jane Welsh and Thomas Carlyle, Effie Gray and John Ruskin, Harriet Taylor and John Stuart Mill, Catherine Hogarth and Charles Dickens, George Eliot and George Henry Lewes—were mostly linked by time and place, but Rose notices a shared quality: their unions were most successful not when they agreed on what was objectively correct, but when they believed the same narrative construct about their love. Marriages end and couples split for many reasons, but as long as we have our story straight, the couple believes, we have an *us*. "To the extent that we impose some narrative form onto our lives, each of us in the ordinary process of living is a fitful novelist," says Rose, a sentence that makes me want to shriek *Phyllis!* every time I think about it.

Nora Ephron once said she read *Parallel Lives* every four or five years, an impulse I understand but a frequency that feels insufficient. I can read a sentence once, considering it insightful but obvious enough; then, on a second or fourth or seventh reading, the same sentence would uncoil itself, revealing something almost unsettlingly perceptive. For example: "It is, of course, one of life's persistent disappointments that a great moral crisis in my life is nothing but matter for gossip in yours." That sentence made me gasp the first time I understood it and makes me want to lie down every time I remember it. Isn't that how it always goes? Your worst moment is someone else's witty anecdote, and vice versa. Most of what we hear this way is too true to be good, in any case. We simplify those stories to match what our imagination is capable of handling. I had always suspected there were two kinds of people in the world: those who will admit to gossiping about the end of a marriage with the same gravity they would bring to ordering appetizers for the table, and liars. *Parallel Lives* is full of statements like that, insights set to stun. In Rose's writing I found company, if not proof. Here was a feeling I knew. Despite our best efforts, nothing happens in or on time. Our memories are made with whats, not whens.

Comparing the stories of how people live is how we discover new ideas about what a good life can look like. We should resist feeling shame about wanting gossip in our books and at our dinner parties, Rose tells us, in the spirit of "good citizenship." A good gossip knows that to hear these tales is not, on its own, invasive. The stories are as much for the couple as for their presumed audience. It is the parapraxes that come out in public—at dinners and over drinks, between the lines of texts—that show us as much as we're capable of seeing. The search for more complex plots in the stories people offer is the search for more ways of being a person. Bad gossips, on the other hand, are just like bad readers: inattentive and unimaginative. They believe that stories exist to be solved and that behavior should be rated bad or good. I cannot help such people and have learned the hard way not to try.

Intimacy is easy. Honesty is much harder. Gossip—in which we reveal what we think is true about love and lust, power and politics, beginnings and endings—is what happens in between. I sometimes wonder what my life would be like if I had found Rose's book earlier, but this is only a fantasy. It would have been nice, of course, to have more time with the permission Rose gave me to love gossip—more seasons to reread it and remember how the same stories change each time they're told. But reading it sooner would not have made me less stupid in marriage or less sad in divorce.

I t was easy, in my first year of being divorced, to convince myself that everyone was talking about their marriages and their
divorces, too. That we were endlessly considering what we
could or should do about the people we did love, we just weren't *in
love* with them. We were not sure that our love felt like love. In the
mornings I left my windows open, and one day I heard my neighbor on his phone outside, pacing back and forth and saying, *Of
course I believe in nonmonogamy in practice, but in theory?* Then he went
back inside and I couldn't hear the rest. A few weeks later I was
walking through the revolving doors of my office building as two
men in suits were coming out, and one was saying to the other, *And
so then I put my wedding ring back on.*

People I know and people I don't tell me their stories unasked.
My social life had taken on the same feeling as work: obligatory en-
joyment. We went to meetings instead of parties and when we did
go to parties it was with the same people from the meetings. There
was no shortage of epiphanies in my world. Everyone was always
realizing something. About themselves, their relationships, their
work, their world. Every night another flash. The realizations were
painful, and valuable, and best of all once we had them they didn't
require us to do anything. They didn't even necessarily have to
be true. Just feeling right was enough. It's not that truth had no

meaning, but that an instance of it had about as much to offer as a well-told lie.

I don't ask the first question, but I find I ask all the questions that follow. There is something about choosing to make divorce the focus of all my attention that seems to free us both: I do not have to talk about mine, and they don't have to pretend not to be thinking about theirs. I accumulate information about first marriages and custody battles and legal anomalies and the first book they read that told them their marriage was over and the divorce movie they've come to identify with most.

Once, a very drunk woman I knew from another life sat down beside me at one of these parties and asked how it could be that the last time she had seen me I was married, and now I wasn't. "So what happened," she said, rather than asked. "You just decided you didn't want to be married? Or was there more to it than that?" There was a great deal more, but I declined to share with her.

One night I went to a work party and a nice young man approached me to say he had recently met my former husband. I blinked twice, as though he'd know that was code for *What's your point?* He took it as an invitation to keep speaking. "He's so nice!" he said. "Yeah," I said as I turned away. "That's why I married him." Later I heard he complained to a mutual friend that my annoyance was unfair. "How was I supposed to know they were on bad terms?" he asked. "They're *divorced*," she told him.

I was married for one year, and with my husband for twelve before that. When we divorced, I was like, *Well, I guess now I'll
date.* I downloaded apps and swiped, although I only ever met
with people I already knew, or who could prove themselves through
mutual acquaintances. I was eager to commiserate with my single
friends—*Hey guys, I have Tinder, too! It sucks! Ha ha*—although for the
most part Tinder was fine. My taste was bad. So many of those
men from that time turned out to be the same. I felt responsible for
my choices even though I often protested I could never have known.
It's not like I looked at them and knew which ones would turn out to
be cruel or hate the taste of coffee. I wanted to try anything until
I had, and then, in the moment, decided I believed it was some sort
of receding thing. What I had wanted was a tangible object that
kept drifting away, light and frail as a weed, entirely out of my
reach.

I slept with a friend who had recently ended his marriage, or
at least I thought he had. The night of, he was *separated*. The next
morning he was *separating*. I have never thought of myself as a particularly moral person, but that kind of disrespect for his spouse
and for verb tenses, I would not stand for.

I dated people who were in more obviously open relationships and
had some of my own. Here's what I know about open relationships:

they're fun until they aren't. Here's what I know about monogamous relationships: the same.

I told everyone I dated I was getting divorced, and paid attention to their responses. Some men were surprised to hear I'd been with the same man for so long, and would respond, "How *old* are you?" I am ten thousand years old, I answered, as though they'd asked how old I felt.

The dates gave some order to my life. If I didn't expect someone to come home with me, I might not clean the piles of papers on my coffee table, might not put on my duvet cover or wash the dishes; I might not moisturize or shave my legs or brush my hair. In this way I was sometimes grateful for the motivation. If it was just me in bed that night, I wouldn't, I thought, have the energy to care.

After a while I started to resent the routine I had made for myself. My own standards seemed punitive, exacting. I never let myself skip a step. I didn't know what I wanted because I spent so much time considering what I could get.

Sometimes the stories we told each other in my clean sheets were sad. Other times the stories were funny. One man told me about a woman who was, it seemed, auditioning him to be the third in her open marriage, which he liked. They had a good time, he said, but when he texted her again she told him she had discussed it with her husband and decided she wasn't into it after all. He asked, claiming to be intrigued rather than hurt, why not. "I don't know," he remembered her replying. "I guess I just think sexual attraction has to be both immutable and ineffable." I laughed; I couldn't help myself—she must have been so hot.

Other men were *into* the idea of me being divorced. They would ask me when I knew my marriage was over. *That's the wrong question,*

I told them, by which I meant, *I know you think there's a right answer.* I could feel how they forced closeness to approximate intimacy. One man told me he thought it was cool, that it must mean I knew so much about relationships. It meant, I thought, the opposite, but I didn't say anything. Immediately after we had sex—not even a breath had elapsed between us—he turned to me and said, *So, how soon after getting married did you know it was over?* My exhale came out like a bark, shocked into yelping by such an intimate question. We had just met.

To be honest, I wasn't that different. I went on a few dates with a man I had worked with, and was delighted to learn that he had been divorced. I sat up straighter, excited to hear more, eager to find someone who was just like me. This man did not think it was cute. "You are the only woman," he said, not without some suspicion, "who has ever responded like that."

I was fascinated by the appliances and fixtures owned by the men I slept with. They seemed to communicate something I needed to know. On a hot night a former coworker invited me to dinner, and I went home with him afterward. All I wanted to do was sleep in a cool bed with a nice man, and my attention kept wandering as he was undressing me. When he turned me around to unzip my dress I wondered if it would kill the mood to say that I could see he had set his air conditioner to sixty-nine degrees, which I thought was funny. He did not think it was funny but he did not let it kill the mood. I slept really well that night.

Another man would invite me over late, even though he often had to leave very early the next morning for work. His phone was connected to a Bluetooth speaker, and he would come into the bedroom to kiss me and I would mutter *Bye-bye*, still mostly asleep, and then as he left I would hear the *bleep bloop* of the Bluetooth disconnecting itself. Like the speaker also wanted to say *Bye-bye*. I thought that was very funny, but never had the occasion to tell him so.

I tried to express to my friend what I think is my ambivalence toward dating: how much I hate being labeled a girlfriend, how I don't want to call a man my boyfriend. "Is this like how sometimes," she started slowly, and I already knew that what she would say next would hurt my feelings, "you can't pick an outfit because you just don't want to go to the party?"

There was a bar we loved back then. It was red and unhappy, a dour subterranean neighborhood institution where nothing could stop us from being charmed by it. Not its stubborn insistence on overhead lighting, not the rotting pink bar of soap in the bathroom, not an overtly hostile approach to fulfilling drink orders. (I once became genuinely concerned when a friend I brought for his first visit tried to ask to see the wine list. "No, no," I nervously interjected when I saw the bartender's jaw tighten. "There's no list. It's house red or house white. Pick one, now, please." He chose the red.)

On one of those nights my friend brought her friend. This friend was, I knew, dating someone I had been involved with. Everyone wanted to hear how that was going. I sank back, hiding my face from the dangling lightbulbs overhead, sipping my house red, to listen.

She fiddled with her hair. She blushed when she spoke. She talked about anything but him. Instead, she started to explain that she had become fixated on the state of her hair color. She wanted to change it. She had decided she would only change it when she knew she was in love.

I felt sick then. Sick in and of that space I was determined to make my own; silently sick beside the crowd of people I was determined to do the same with. I was sick with jealousy, and loneliness, and longing. She was already in love. Anyone could see that even without the lightbulbs. The next time I saw her, her hair would be a different color, and I would know what that meant to her. More than that, I felt sure he loved her, too. Even more: she thought of her love as something that she gave and expressed on her terms, not as something that she could receive only when offered. She was in love as a feeling, not as a form of belonging.

During the first spring of my separation I spent some time with a man I liked. He would leave bed late at night and come back with a plum cut into quarters, make me follow him to the backyard, where he would try to convince me that we should both smoke naked. *What if the neighbors see!* I protested, but barely. *It's too dark!* he insisted. It was night, true, but the sky was bright and purple, even more so when considered behind the red glow of a lit cigarette. Back inside he would run his fingers over my thighs, pull my legs across his body, ask me to stay with him like that for hours.

His wife had died the year before. Sometime after the cigarettes but before the sun came up he would want to talk about what we had in common. We were the same age, and we felt our ages multiplying inside us. We had both been with our partners for over a decade. We had both been unsure about marriage, which was our safe way of admitting we had married for reasons more practical than passionate. We had both loved our weddings, loved the memory of them. We were both, he pointed out, trying to live as adults on our own for the first time years after our friends, at colleges and in new cities, had done the same.

He was insistent that we were both grieving, and he did not think his grief was any worse than mine. I knew he wasn't being literal. The feeling of divorce follows a grieving process. Death is grief. I think he just wanted someone to be with him, and he took similarities where he could find them. His experience had made him incidentally compassionate—misplaced, but sincere. I spent all spring considering his care. Sometimes sensitive people are so much so, they cannot imagine anyone ever feeling the way they do. He instead hoped that if he felt this way someone else did as well. What he wanted most was to say and to hear, *Hey, me too.*

Self-help books about mourning and horror movies about ghosts understand the same thing: grief opens the direction of our minds, takes us to ideas that might have seemed strange in the light of earlier days. Suddenly we're willing to recite incantations to raise the dead, or affirmations to raise our self-esteem. We are lost to the cursed idea of closure, thinking the people who can help us are the people who hurt us. A week earlier maybe we would have said we didn't believe in the afterlife, or hardcovers featuring pop psychologists crossing their arms under an embossed title. Then we lost the quality of certainty—now we see how stupid that certainty was—and so who can say what's real and what's possible? Not us.

In those conversations about grief, I would concede that we shared something: we were both somehow too early and too late for our experiences. We mourned something lots of people knew, but they couldn't yet hear what we most wanted to say. A decade ago we committed while our friends were single. A decade from now, we agreed, there would be more of our friends like us. Though we wanted to spare them pain, we knew that one day they'd feel like we did. They would share our status as former spouses. They would lose who they loved, by choice or by fate. Our experiences would be common, even if they would never be ordinary. But we would always be out of time.

Time concerned me a lot, then. It still does now.

III

My two friends in love seemed to always be rearranging their apartment. Every time I went over, the couch we'd chosen was in a different place. They got a dog, and he was very cute. No matter where the new couch was in their living room, I always wanted to be sitting on it, drinking their whiskey and petting their dog. "Have you heard from Dylan?" they would ask me as we tested the recently installed light fixtures.

Dylan. Yes. I heard from him often. My friend had introduced us, almost by accident; he had been invited to a birthday party she organized for a mutual friend. Over the years of our friendship I had heard her talk about him, knew that when they were young they had been very much in love and that they still were, in a different way. They seemed like a model for exes. When I met him I was ready to like him very much; this instinct, when I was in the mood for romance, seemed prophetic. When I was not in the mood this instinct seemed only self-fulfilling.

I liked Dylan. Dylan, I heard, liked me, too. We went for drinks. We fucked. We still liked each other. We began to see each other with some regularity: every few weeks, every other week. Dylan had lived in the city for longer than I had, knew where to find what I couldn't. He knew what was fun. He saw other people and so did I. Dating! I thought.

Dylan had been one of those children who don't speak at all until they're toddlers, and then suddenly start speaking in complete sentences. His parents were concerned, until one day he was three years old and, in his backyard, casually remarked that a four-syllable word for aircraft was flying overhead. When he told me that story I understood much more about why he spoke and texted the way he did. His syntax, whether in speech or writing, was always closer to the way thoughts feel than sentences are supposed to sound. He wouldn't say anything for long stretches and then when he spoke he would say something so odd I couldn't help it, I was in love with him. Once he texted to say he was thinking about the inside of my wrists; another time, the space that floated immediately around my cheekbones. *I want to fuck you on a glacier*, he texted me once. *You want to fuck me on a block of ice?* I texted back, kind of laughing to myself at the idea. He always seemed to be thinking of textures and temperatures. You want to be naked on a melting sheet of frozen water? *I want to be more alone with you than seems possible*, he explained. *Oh*, I thought, *that's ridiculous, I love you.*

I didn't say it. Instead some mornings, after really good nights, I would pace in my living room, crying just a little. "Please sit down," he would plead from the couch, and I would refuse because I wanted that too much. Nothing good can come from wanting. "Please don't go," I would say in response, and he would lean forward with his hand covering his mouth and his eyebrows pulling together as he considered the best way to tell me to *stop*, to just stop, please. "You look so hot when you're concerned," I told him once, which made him laugh, but he did. I am most attracted to men when they are concentrating. When they work and when they worry, they make the same face. I would reassure him I was fine, I was sorry, and he would leave. I was always convinced that that was the last time I'd see him. He always texted me first.

When we met he was a chef for a catering company favored by movie stars who required the waitstaff to sign nondisclosure agreements, or sometimes he would prepare meals that went untouched by politicians, who usually ate at McDonald's on the way to the party. Their security detail preferred it, he explained to me. There was a lower risk of poison.

Often he would come home with the strangest assortment of leftovers and keep cooking. *Can I help?* I'd ask, and he would give me bread to slice or vegetables to chop, and when I handed him the results on a board, embarrassed at my inelegance compared to his dexterity, he was always kind. *They're rustic cut,* he would say.

One week I was asked to participate in a reading series where everyone must bring a piece of writing that makes them cry. I chose "Wants" by Grace Paley, a short story about a woman who bumps into her ex-husband at the library, where she is returning some overdue books. Reading it made me sad, but not really a crying sad. Mostly it was the kind of story that held my exhales. I thought that was close enough. I brought it to Dylan's house, because he had invited me over for dinner. "Want me to read you this story while you're cooking?" I asked, wanting to practice and to entertain him, and he said yes while he stirred a pot on the stove.

"I saw my ex-husband in the street," I started. "I was sitting on the steps of the new library. Hello, my life, I said. We had once been married for twenty-seven years, so I felt justified. He said, What? What life? No life of mine. I said, O.K., I don't argue when there's real disagreement."

I had made a mistake and I had been right, I knew immediately;

the story, about a formerly married couple sharing different memories of their mornings, was going to make me cry. The husband says he wanted a sailboat, but the wife, he says—she didn't want anything.

I stopped. Dylan stopped stirring. There were tears on his countertop. We looked at each other and I looked at my book. I read what the husband says to his wife: *You'll always want nothing.*

Paley writes:

He had had a habit throughout the twenty-seven years of making a narrow remark which, like a plumber's snake, could work its way through the ear down the throat, half-way to my heart. He would then disappear, leaving me choking with equipment.

Dylan left the stove and stood beside me while I cried and read. My breaths were swallowing the words but I was definitely going to finish.

But I do want something. . . . I wanted to have been married forever to one person, my ex-husband or my present one. Either has enough character for a whole life, which as it turns out is really not such a long time. You couldn't exhaust either man's qualities or get under the rock of his reasons in one short life.

I wiped the tears from my face and said nothing. I would have asked for death before I'd ask for a tissue. Dylan turned my shoulders so I was facing him, and he took my wet face in his hands. "Maybe you should read something else," he said.

I stopped seeing other people, and told him so. He kept seeing other people and told me so. For a while this seemed fine. One night it didn't. We were in bed and I made deals with myself: *When I count to three I'll tell him I love him. When I count to five I'll tell him I love him. Five thousand and I'll tell him I love him.* "Your breathing feels kind of crazy?" he said, as though it were a question. It did. I could tell he wanted nothing more than for me to exhale, and I would not give him that satisfaction. "Listen, I love you," I told him. "Oh," he said, and in the dark I couldn't tell if he was relieved—*That's all?*—or upset—*Oh no*—and then he said, "I love you." I was happy then, happy and scared, and the next morning I made toast and eggs with nervous hands. The power went out for no reason we could tell and the toaster stopped working and I stood there for awhile, thinking, before he gently suggested that he could toast the bread in the same pan as the eggs while I called my super, and when I came back he cut the bread in two and handed me breakfast on a plate. I had made the eggs the way I like them, soft, but I worried he wouldn't think I was cute anymore if he saw me dripping yolk, which I knew I would because my hands were still shaking. When he left he said I love you, again, before I said it, and he turned around to smile before I closed the door behind him. Later, after it was over, he mentioned that morning. *That morning was special*, he said. That morning was a disaster, I thought.

I'll romanticize a lot of things, but not this time when I was divorced and trying to be anything else, like a woman in love. This time has had none of the features of romance. What are those? Anticipation, wanting, electricity. This time was dull, static, dread. Romance in reverse is . . . what? Heartstill. Like heartbreak but with an absence of beating. In *Pitch Dark*, a Renata Adler novel I love and was reading at the time, the main character is having an affair with a married man. She describes a night when her lover showing up with his dog moved her "not to tears, I guess, but to a stillness of the heart." Like that.

One day Dylan visited to tell me that things were over with the other woman he was seeing. At least, they were about to be over. He planned to have it be over soon. I was flat on my back and half-undressed before I asked him to wait and while he waited I sat up a little to ask, on my elbows: *Just to be clear, nothing has changed?* He also sat up, the better to consider his answer. "Well," he said, gesturing between us, "I think we've changed."

I broke up with him very soon after, which was a surprise to both of us. I had known I was considering it but didn't know I had made a decision until I was on his couch, my arms stiff by my side. I knew my heart was broken but I didn't know that would make it so open. I loved him at a moment when I was convinced I would never love anyone like that again. Now that doesn't seem as contradictory as it did then; now it seems like it was only possible because I was so convinced I couldn't. I cried and he put his forehead in the space between my neck and my collarbone—some mornings, before he left, he would say *I want to spend my day right here* and point to exactly that spot—and I cried more. I broke up with him because his few words and even fewer complete sentences weren't adding up, although he insisted I was mistaken, insisted I was misunderstanding, wanted to know why, if we were in love, we had to break up. I didn't have a good answer. Was I just reading him wrong? I remembered that only a few weeks before, he had left me standing alone outside a bar for reasons he wouldn't explain. I watched him walk out of my sight, his hands pulling at his hair. I had been a woman slowly walking backward on the sidewalk, watching him walk forward out of my sight—his legs turned into shadows, his hands pulling at his hair. He had walked around the corner and I had crossed my arms to give myself the strength to turn around and walk forward in my own direction, thought *If you would just ask I would say yes* so loudly it seemed like he should have heard.

We never did fuck on a glacier, but it was true that when we were together we seemed more alone with each other than I would have thought possible. He used to hold my head in both his hands so that when I was underneath him one palm would press against the back of my neck and the other hand would curl his fingers through my hair, and I would tip my throat up and he would lean his face down and say, with his lips on mine, *I can't get close enough.* I knew what he meant, or what he wanted, and I was sorry, but not sorry enough to get any closer than we were in those moments.

The night I broke up with him, the air was so hot. I had worn my favorite dress, navy blue and the kind of thin silk that skims the skin, which I like mostly because of the sound it makes when I take it off and drop it on the floor. When he kissed me I stopped crying, and when he took my dress off I stopped breathing, the soft thump I had promised myself better than oxygen. When his hands were against me, his fingers aligned to my ribs, I started exhaling again. Every breath sounded like *iloveyouiloveyouiloveyouiloveyou* but my lips never moved. I loved him I loved him I loved him.

I left so quickly I bumped into his doorframe on the way out. The next day at work I noticed the bruise on my arm, creeping down past my T-shirt sleeve. "How did you get that?" a friend asked me. I didn't know what to say.

A memory would often surface during this time, something that had happened the previous summer. I had gone home to pack up my old apartment. I knew then I wanted to end my marriage but it was still months before I would say so out loud. My thoughts were lost and I was walking slowly, overwhelmed by trying to keep them still while avoiding the garbage cans that took up entire city blocks. I kept my head down, and when a man's voice started yelling for my attention I ignored it as long as I could. He was parking a car, I could tell out of the corner of my eye, and yelling out his window, *Hey baby, aren't you far from home? No,* I yelled back, even in my rage unable to tell a lie—I was blocks away from the almost-empty apartment I would be leaving in a few days. "Haley, I know you're far from home," he said, and I stopped to look up. "You live in New York now," he continued, getting out of the car, and I saw it was a man I used to work with, the ex-boyfriend of another coworker.

Everyone in the office had often remarked on the way he looked like old photos of character actors; the planes of his face seemed to belong to another decade, his mannerisms from another era. He had been a sincere and loving boyfriend, but these good qualities were like his curse. His love was intense and possessive—too much for the kind of women he tended to fall in love with, like the woman we had worked with. At the time I think he was still in love with her. Since then I have come across many more instances of this type of man: the one who finds happiness in getting hold of a woman who hates to be held.

I got mad for a minute, reminding him that he can't shout at women out of car windows when they're walking home late at night, that he hadn't scared me, exactly, but he could have. I forgave him for his apologies and his cigarettes.

He walked me home and I could tell he wanted to ask about his ex but wouldn't. Whatever he said had the charge of wanting credit for his restraint and the reward of information offered, not requested. We stopped to buy more cigarettes and hesitated in conversation when we got to my front door. I looked up and saw the lights were on in my house, looked at him and saw the way distance was working between us. He would have done anything to get closer to his ex; in that moment I would have done anything to get farther from the man waiting inside. We paused, and I wondered what could happen next, as though it wasn't my choice to make. It felt like a long time before we stubbed out our cigarettes and said good night.

M y husband and I were very different in high school. He was an excellent student, popular with everyone. He ran for student council and won; he was valedictorian and prom king the year we graduated. I was uncomfortable and shy, uninterested in grades and, for that matter, most classes. If I liked a teacher, or liked the subject, I did fine. I was almost always on the verge of failing. The only extracurricular I did, in my first three years, was makeup for the school's many elaborate theatrical performances.

When we began dating I changed myself into someone who cared a little. I worked on the newspaper, I went to the assemblies, I spoke to people I didn't know.

He wanted to be a filmmaker and got into a good university. I wanted to be a writer, at first, and then all of a sudden I wanted nothing. I got into a journalism program and dropped out after a few weeks. I slept through mornings, worked retail in the afternoons and evenings. He would come pick me up and we would spend the night in his room, a basement without windows. I re-enrolled at another university and took maybe two classes a semester for a few years, in between shifts at whatever clothing store had hired me. I was frustrated and, in retrospect, very depressed.

I found his education incredible. He and his friends were learning to make what they loved. They spent hours watching movies, and talking about them. Their technical classes contained details I had never thought of before, and have never forgotten since. The wet streets of outdoor nighttime shoots, to reflect light; the pallets of wood loaded into the rented trucks to make rickety dollies for practicing cinematographers. "Everyone wants a dolly shot," my husband would tell me when preparing for a shoot. One of his friends would talk frequently about the rules of light and shadow, how he was noticing that what their teachers told them was best was often not what made for the most beautiful movies. On his sets, he wanted to illuminate darkness instead of eliminating it. The women in the program wrote bizarre, hilarious screenplays about people addicted to tanning beds, or practiced different sound techniques, forever carrying enormous bags of supplies for some baroque method of replicating noise.

I wanted to be that skilled and that smart. The only work that had made me really happy—or better than happy, sure that I knew what I was doing—was when I was backstage at those school plays, painting faces and pulling hair. I decided to go to makeup school.

This time, part-time school didn't bother me; this time, I was obsessed with what I learned. The teachers were beautiful women with long and soft hair that brushed against our arms when they demonstrated techniques on us during lectures. They had spent years on film sets or television shows. One teacher was the makeup artist for a local morning news program, and would come to teach our class after her four a.m. to twelve p.m. shift ended. They introduced us to tiny stores hidden up several flights of stairs, where we were expected to buy specific German brands of paste for eyebrow blocking, or a particularly preferred shade of brown cake liner.

The details, again, were what thrilled me. I learned to shape a face with different colors of foundation, to choose the right brush for the right texture. I took classes in practical versions of special effects: no monsters or anything, just basic wounds. On my own hand I would mold putty into the shape of a bullet wound, paint over it with foundation, pool the two types of blood necessary to make it look real—a thick, dark blood that settled inside the hollow of the mold, and then the liquid blood that would drip down to the paper towel I laid beneath my station. On the other hand I would make a bad burn, or an aging bruise.

I began working at makeup counters in a nearby department store and loved the authority the customers gave to me and my co-workers. If I recommended a product, they bought it; when I applied it, they complained, saying they would never be able to do it so well themselves when they took it home. That's not true! I reassured them. It's just practice.

I wanted the experience and I wanted to be with my husband and I wanted the acceptance of his friends and so I offered to do the makeup for their fourth-year films. In the mornings, while it was still dark, I would apply my own makeup in his tiny bathroom, and pack my kit while he showered. We would drive to sets together, where he did the sound, holding the boom for hours or hunched over dials that, when explained to me, had applications so precise their instructions seemed esoteric. I laid out my station and tilted the chins of the students from the theater department, filled in their brows and pressed primer onto their cheeks. I would hold up my index finger a few inches from their face, just to the left of their nose, and tell them to look there so that I could properly apply shadow to the crease of their eyelids, which is better done when the eyes are half-open than fully closed. During shooting, I silently cleaned my brushes on paper towels laid out in front of me, careful not to let the table underneath them squeak.

The sets got more elaborate. Many were overnight, in alleyways or office buildings, when we could be guaranteed uninterrupted hours of night for outdoor shots, or many uninterrupted hours of fluorescent-lit cubicles. Then we would go back to motels to pull the blinds and sleep until it was time for breakfast in the late afternoon and ride back to the location at sunset. There was one particularly beautiful, surreal short film that was shot in the small town where the director had grown up. He introduced us to what seemed like the entire population and his whole family over the course of four days. "This is my uncle," he would say. "He's also head of the fire department." The next day his uncle came back to the shoot to supervise; the scene required a bonfire.

This movie was about a soldier trapped in some kind of endless dream war, and it finally required me to use what I had learned about burn techniques on the actor's jaw and neck. I took Polaroids to show my classmates, proud to have proof of my education at work. My husband, after months of straining his back holding the boom, hurt himself badly, and in the mornings we all took care of him, helping him reach his socks or carrying his equipment. At night, we drank beer and watched horror movies. That was the first time I saw *The Thing*. The Rob Bottin makeup, the Stan Winston puppets—the practical effects, the way the monster moved through the Antarctic—are still my favorite.

I considered this work to be practice for real life, and it made me happy. I didn't know about the next eight years that were ahead of us—that I would not end up working as a makeup artist, for one—and in many ways didn't care. I didn't know then about the first apartment my husband and I would move into, the kind of place that a real estate agent might have called a "starter rental." I found it on a classifieds website. Small, nondescript, its most memorable feature was that it was walking distance from the bars our friends most liked to frequent.

The second apartment was only down the street but worlds better than the first. It was a ground-level without much light, we had access to the large backyard through our bedroom, and from our front door we walked out directly to the best park in the neighborhood. We always knew when spring was really here because the courts at the edge of the park would, every single day starting at five p.m., be filled with older men playing volleyball while their families watched. Inside, we had a big bed, a small white corner desk I had found at a secondhand store, a large computer monitor we used to watch movies and television shows, a couch with an ottoman to stretch our legs—it all seemed like such abundant good luck.

It was in this apartment that our circle of friends grew wider and closer all at once. I started a new job at a boutique with a staff of people I found hilarious, beautiful, elegant—they had a sense of taste I could only aspire to from the office upstairs, where I did the paperwork, or the basement, where I kept track of the merchandise. They had loud laughs and incredible shoes. The store manager used to throw her own parties periodically and all of them, no matter how casual, were like something out of an interior design magazine. When she cooked dinner she would explain to everyone how to take a little of everything on the plate on a fork to create the absolute perfect bite. We would happily do whatever she told us; she was always right.

The friends we had for the longest time moved to our neighborhood, renting a duplex apartment that became the place we started and ended every weekend night. We had a playlist that began to feel almost Pavlovian—this song for when we were putting on our makeup, that song when it was time to call cabs and get to the bar. To this day I still experience a full-body cringe, my entire torso contracting, when I hear Animal Collective or Wolf Parade. God help anyone who tries to put on LCD Soundsystem.

There were so many parties, and people moved in and out of the rooms there so much that it began to take on the feeling of a family home, one where everyone was expected to show their face at least once a month. One summer afternoon my friend invited me over to help her bake cupcakes to bring to her boyfriend's family's Shabbat dinner, a minor yet important occasion to be invited over for. Her boyfriend and I teased her about how she would need, in order to be fully embraced by his Jewish mother, to subtly guilt her as she accepted this gift. "Tell her that you spent *the hottest day of the year* absolutely *slaving* over the hot stove," we counseled.

"I'm not going to do that," she told us, wisely.

Later I found out that her boyfriend had tried to do it on her behalf. "Hey, Mom," he said as she took a cupcake for dessert. "Did you know my girlfriend made these cupcakes *just for you* on the *hottest day of the year*?"

Apparently without missing a beat, she had responded: "Aren't I worth it?"

Those warm months were when we would gather at the park, watching the never-ending volleyball game, surreptitiously drinking beer out of half-rinsed iced coffee cups, talking shit and getting sunburns. I would toss people my keys and they would run to pee at our place—keeping that apartment neat, now that I'm thinking about it, was also based on knowing how frequently people would be walking through my bedroom.

That was also the time I started working lots of different jobs. I had left an office job at a law firm, convinced that twenty-five was some kind of hard deadline for my entire life. While that turned out not to be true, the motivation was probably for the best. My job at the boutique started most days at ten a.m. (earlier when the owner would go on buying trips and I would have to work on Paris or Milan time, wait by the fax machine for her to send back her selects so I could enter them into our spreadsheets, and then by the time she was on her way to dinner it was early afternoon and I was free for the day). I began volunteering for an independent fashion magazine on the weekends, and that's where I made some of the longest-running friendships of my life so far. I learned how to be a freelance writer from those women, and started pitching often and getting assignments sometimes.

I worked constantly, both at home and at the offices for the store and the magazine, occasionally at a coffee shop between our apartment and the store. I woke up most days before six a.m., to write and make to-do lists and check things off. I was run down and frequently suffering from a persistent cough or cold but I loved it. I loved feeling like my days were full and my mind was occupied.

Some days my husband would come to the store and pick me up so we could walk home together. We often teased my boss, who was very open about finding him charming and good-looking. My husband was, like me, really good at flirting, and their banter became a constant joke among my coworkers and me. What if my boss ended up stealing my husband? What a great story that would be, we said.

One evening I came downstairs and found him holding my boss's large purse and her dog on a leash. "What are you doing?" I asked, the joke becoming true in front of me. He gestured at my boss talking to another business owner across the street; he had just wanted to be nice, he said.

At night, if I was ready to stop working, we would invite friends over. I felt as though some previously fractured elements in my life were being put back in place. Many of my friends were in the process of taking apart what they thought they wanted, starting jobs in unexpected fields or ending the relationships they had held on to throughout and beyond university. For a few years I had been sensitive to the way it was a little unusual that my husband and I were so committed to each other. We stood in obvious contrast to the more typical ways our friends were going through the phases of meeting people, getting attached, cycling through different ways of leaving a person. I felt insecure about this most of the time; maybe all the time. But when I thought about really being single my mind treated it like any other unobtainable daydream, something I imagined based on what I saw but couldn't guess how it would feel to have.

My husband broke up with me in earnest once, before we lived together and right after he graduated film school. He was introduced to a friend of a friend at a party we both attended. She was unnaturally and undeniably beautiful—I can still see her cheekbones, high and full in a way that made her look both serious and like she was always smiling—but more important, as he explained carefully the morning he came over to end things with me, she really understood film. I panicked and begged, which didn't work, and after he left I paced endlessly. A friend took me to a mall we liked downtown, and we leaned over the banisters and stared up at the skylights or down at the escalators endlessly dropping people off onto the lower levels. "Maybe it's for the best," she said. "I hate you," I said, and really meant it.

My husband came back three days later, ashamed and repentant. I forgave him and mostly forgot. It was only much later that I remembered how it had been that third afternoon when I first started to really hear my friend's voice saying, *Maybe it's for the best*, that my sisters and I had walked to get iced coffees and brought them home to watch bad television in bed, that I had made plans that night with friends he didn't know as well, that I had decided to go to the library the next day for new books to read. I would have gotten over it then, I realized years after the fact, when I started understanding I would have to get over it now in a much different way.

In our second apartment I felt like I could be a little more spontaneous, a little less overscheduled; not often, but sometimes. One Saturday became a true day off after a morning working—my husband and I had lunch, walked around our neighborhood, I bought a pair of vintage shoes at a favorite store. On the way out, thin brown paper bag in hand, we bumped into our friends Lisa and Sarah, who had just moved in together not too far away. They were also having a spontaneous Saturday off. We invited them over for dinner, taking our plates to the backyard and talking fast about all the things we wanted to tell each other.

Lisa was in a bad situation with her good friends, a close and secure group that I often felt like a fan of. Meeting them had only confirmed that feeling. They were smart in ways I was just starting to learn to value: educated, sure, but mostly they were curious. It seemed like they were incapable of boredom. They dressed themselves in real outfits, obviously ones they had considered from head to toe, but with the ease that lets you know it was a natural extension of how they saw themselves. Those were the years when I was realizing how important a quality it was for a person to look like themselves, that when I looked at someone and thought they were beautiful what I was really seeing was that they knew who they were.

With this sense of self came, it seemed, a very definitive idea of what their lives should be. Two of these friends had been dating each other, and it was taken for granted that once together they would stay that way forever. When their idea of a life diverged, they broke up. This choice seemed, in Lisa's description, all the more devastating because it was so practical. Knowing it was right or for the best didn't change this moment, now, when the family that they had built was experiencing a shift not unlike any of their parents' divorces or any other they had witnessed in other families as children. They were unmoored by it, adrift. Lisa was mostly concerned about how to be a good friend to both—how to be there for one without feeling like it would betray the other. I heard what had happened as something between rumor and experience. It would never be our story to tell, but it had changed something about our lives to be near it.

We thought about this for a while, until Sarah and my husband pointed out that a large pack of raccoons was also contemplating our conversation from the roof above our heads, and so we decided to concede the backyard to them and call it a night.

When an apartment on the second floor opened up we took it, a slightly larger space and way, way more natural light. The previous tenants had left a long, dark wood table that fit perfectly as a divider between the living room and the kitchen. Here I did a little more decorating, accepting a friend's glass coffee table she was getting rid of in a move, bringing home bookshelves from yard sales and buying prints from a beloved art bookstore. I often worked the tables when the fashion magazine went to zine fairs, and there I would trade back issues of the magazine for large, screen-printed posters or hand-drawn postcards. I spent a long time arranging and taping what I gathered on the walls, like I had as a teenager, but this time, I hoped, with slightly more mature taste. In the bedroom I put a white shag rug beside the bed, like I had seen in interior design magazines. I only hung one piece of art on the wall in that room, a reflective silver square that said, in big black letters, "Pleasure Is Forever." But really, then just like now, all I cared about was the books, and I had systems for keeping track of which piles were being read, which ones were for work and research, which ones passed through my shelves to friends, and which ones were borrowed in turn.

My husband had been working the same job for a long time, and had a good thing at his company. I was still working multiple jobs, staying on at the clothing store to help with things like payroll and special events, freelancing whenever I could, taking odd jobs to write copy or do data entry just to make extra money; anything to support working for the fashion magazine, which I loved too much despite the fact that—or maybe because—it was a job that couldn't pay me anything at all. I began to know other women in a way I hadn't since I was a teenager—obsessively, joyously finding out more about them, spending hours and hours with them in our apartments. My mornings were for deadlines; my evenings were for friends; in between the hours were filled with what I needed to do and where I wanted to be.

But the more reasons I had to stay home, the more reasons I found to leave. The magazine, at its ten-year anniversary, shut down, and I got another job in another city, another country. While I waited for my visa to go through, I would visit this new city, New York, at least once a month, staying on friends' couches and before falling asleep calling my husband to tell him about my day. On one of those nights my friend Nic sat beside me while I Skyped my husband and told him what my lawyers had suggested, if we wanted to move at the same time. *Well, I guess we should get married*, I said, and though we had already talked about that as a possibility, now, in my memory, it seems like the closest we came to a proposal—that I had asked, and he had answered. That we did so without ceremony or even privacy, let alone in person, did not bother me then. It doesn't exactly bother me now. I only still wonder what my proposal meant, if anything at all. The visa was approved one of those nights away, the email arriving right before I went to sleep on a favorite couch, and I left knowing that the next time I came back to New York it would be the first time I would be coming home.

When things with my husband were good it had the feeling of being away. It was a desperate exaltation of believing that a vacation self is a true self, and the one at home is the fraud. *Let's stay here forever*, I'd want to say, but I had no idea where "here" was. When things were bad, though, it didn't feel like being home. More like that momentum that drags one to the suitcase, the car, the train, the plane—the split between the mind shouting *Turn back* while the feet continue toward an unwanted destination.

My husband's parents—divorced soon after we moved into our first apartment, about five years after my parents divorced—had gotten married when they were ready to leave their home country for work, too. On weekend visits to my husband's childhood home I would find a framed picture that was placed a little behind the photos of my husband and his sister as children, images of them in shorts and striped T-shirts with facial expressions that read as mischievous in that sweet, devious way smart and well-loved kids have. It was impossible to tell if that's what their expressions actually were or if that's just how I came to see them after ten years of hearing the stories about all their irrepressibly scampy behavior growing up. The picture I looked for was from my in-laws' wedding dinner, their faces in profile as they kissed each other, my mother-in-law's lips very slightly smiling.

Our wedding happened in that living room, the framed photos carefully pushed back to make space for the candlesticks my friends brought with them, the champagne glasses abandoned on corners too close to the edge. That party only happened because of our friends—they brought photos and made a guest book, cooked the food and served it to our families, insisted on doing the hora with dining room chairs, ran the last-minute emergency errands (my husband forgot to bring the pants for his suit, and Lisa had to be dispatched to retrieve them for him before the ceremony started).

Our parents tactfully but tensely avoided their ex-spouses, though interactions between other family members were inevitable. My aunt had spent all evening talking to everyone about a pair of incredible heels she had bought just for the wedding, and at one point my father's new girlfriend had used that as a way into a conversation. "I like your shoes," she tried, the terse attempt quiet but meaning well. My aunt sighed, referred to her as a word for women that has become more common recently yet still has a fair amount of shock value, and walked away. My father, when his girlfriend turned to him for an explanation as to what had just happened, shrugged.

One friend with a fancy camera had been put in charge of the night's photos. She took a picture that, when I saw it, seemed just like our version of the one showing my in-laws kissing at their wedding: a black-and-white shot of us right after the brief ceremony finished and I had said *yeah* in my drawn-out way that made everyone laugh, my white jacket falling off my shoulders, face tilted up as my husband kissed me very lightly, and my lips smiling just a little, happy that I had answered with the airiness of how easy it was to swear I would want what I had. I found something peaceful in how total this promise was. I could leave, I realized then, but I would never, ever be without him again.

Was every married couple two children playing house? Did it just feel that way for us, or was it a pantomime for everyone? There was an endless supply of fictions to choose from, the facts of one not enough to make us lose faith in another. Pretending or daydreaming as a child had had such a prophetic quality, as though adult life could only ever confirm or diverge from fate. In my twenties I often thought about whether my teenage self would be impressed with my life. By my thirties I had remembered that my teenage self was very stupid.

But there is something childlike to these questions about whether to marry, why marry, how to be married, in the way very young kids can see a scene for what it could be rather than what it is. The kind of vision that lets you keep wanting because you haven't seen anything else yet, the kind of patience that follows real hope. We were playing at making decisions. We married at an age when we still believed life happened to us, as though it was for us to observe. This was the age right before we started to wonder if we might be what was happening to our lives, as though it was for us to decide.

When I was twenty-two, all I could imagine of a future was one that kept us together. Maybe, I dreamed, my husband and I would keep working on film sets together like we had when he was a student, or work in the same industry on different projects. At that time he was reading *Easy Riders, Raging Bulls*, Peter Biskind's history of Hollywood in the 1970s and the invention of an American auteur model of filmmaking, and we watched the movies of that era that he was curious about, though many of them failed to move me. I read *Easy Riders, Raging Bulls*, too, and memorized the gossip contained in that reporting the same way I collected techniques on film sets. It all seemed like knowledge I needed, though it wasn't as if I thought it would prove useful, exactly. I just wanted to know. I liked reading about those sets and those directors more than I liked their movies—I remember being especially confused by the cruelty of *Five Easy Pieces*—but then there were some I loved, like *Chinatown*. I wanted to watch it again and again, which was something we fought about: I had little interest in watching many different kinds of new movies. There was something partly superstitious about this. The mood of a movie could influence me very much, and I believed the opposite was true, that if I watched the wrong movie in the wrong mood I wouldn't even really see it. When I found one I loved I just wanted to watch it on repeat.

One evening during the year of my separation, the weather was such that I put on a large, soft tan sweatshirt with thin sweatpants and black backless mules to walk to a movie theater. On the way there I was a few steps behind a boy and a girl who were heading in the same direction. *You have to trust other people*, he said as he dropped his banana peel into the trash. *Oh, I don't trust other people*, she said. *Then you have to trust luck*, he replied. She said: *I definitely don't trust luck! And not your luck, that's for sure.*

I was early—always early—and went into a bookstore nearby to look, trying to remember my list of books I'd been meaning to buy. When enough time had passed I met three friends for a showing of *Waiting to Exhale*, the 1995 movie about four friends experiencing very different stages of grief over the men in their lives. The most famous scene is of Angela Bassett setting her soon-to-be-ex-husband's car on fire in anger (this is my first-favorite divorce movie that begins with a car on fire), though when I rewatch the movie now I always think about the scene right after, when the fire department arrives and she is calmly, simply smoking a cigarette while the television plays behind her. Then there is Whitney Houston in love with a married man, confusing aloneness with loneliness; Lela Rochon trusting the wrong men, constantly bargaining with herself;

Loretta Devine in denial, still in love, even though her husband has come out and is in a relationship with a man.

Written by Terry McMillan, *Exhale* is part of her own canon of divorce literature. As a teenager I had watched her infamous interview with Oprah on live television, too young to have seen *How Stella Got Her Groove Back* but somehow the right age to watch her interrogate the man its romance was based on. When I did finally watch *Stella* I saw an obvious precursor to *Eat Pray Love*, in its luxurious travel interspersed with deep wells of emotional despair, as well as an aura of melodrama in its tragic deaths and questions of whether a young man would really want to be with a woman older than him, much like in Douglas Sirk's 1955 movie, *All That Heaven Allows*.

The real story, of course, turned much more complicated: McMillan had met Jonathan Plummer on vacation in Jamaica. She was forty-three and he was twenty. They spent five days together, and after a few months of talking on the phone post-vacation, she invited him to visit. They married, and stayed married for six years, until Plummer came out and they divorced. Their breakup was a bad one, with both using the media for their own ends and McMillan even suing Plummer for emotional distress damages of $45 million. The 2005 episode of *Oprah* featured McMillan accusing Plummer of intentionally deceiving her, something she apologized for in a 2010 episode, acknowledging that her anger had taken over. The movie adaptations of her works, much like the difference between Ephron's novel *Heartburn* and the film, retain a little bit of that sadness and hurt and anger, but soften it by shortening the length of time between catharsis and the pain that incited it.

The theater for *Exhale* was full of women in groups like ours—almost all threes and fours—and it had the feeling of a shadow play, everyone in the audience yelling the lines they remembered, cheering for the scenes they knew were coming. The man Whitney Houston is in love with is played by Dennis Haysbert, who has been on a lot of television shows and in a lot of movies but I, like most people in the theater, it seemed, recognized him mostly as the spokesperson for Allstate insurance commercials. In the scene when Whitney Houston finally breaks up with him, he accuses her of basically conspiring with his wife. "What," he asks rhetorically, "do you and my wife work for the same firm?"

"State Farm?" someone in the audience yelled.

Afterward we walked down the street to the corner with the bookstore on one side, a bar on the other, a restaurant across the street, pausing to decide where to go next. In front of us a man was lighting matches and blowing them out, making the whole block smell like a birthday.

I went back into the bookstore and walked around, now that I had remembered the book I meant to buy. An event had just ended. The folding chairs were being stacked to one side by the staff; an author was sitting behind a table, talking to the last people there. I turned one corner to see if the book was in a certain section; I turned around to try a different shelf. I saw, very slowly, that the man I had been seeing in the spring was there, the man with the cigarettes in the backyard and the plums in his bedroom and the feeling of not being part of time. He was standing beside the cookbooks.

"Hi," I said, for a second wondering if he would remember me. He asked what I was doing there and I told him I had seen a movie down the street. I asked him the same. His girlfriend knew the author of the book, he explained.

Things had not ended well for us. They had not really ended at all. The last night we saw each other we had both been more than a little combative, maybe hostile, for reasons I don't want to think too deeply about. He had admonished me for seeing a movie he thought was too stupid to pay for, and I had been insulted when he suggested I see more of the movies that played at prestigious repertory cinemas. "I'm a *film critic*," I had snapped. (I am not.) I made predictions for the future: I told him I thought he would remarry within the year, and that I never would. He did not think this was true.

Our last night had not gone well for other reasons, too. He had asked me questions I thought he knew the answers to; he was confusing me with other women. He couldn't remember how many sisters I had or what I did for work, but he did text me later to say he had found my earrings on his nightstand. *A pearl, set in gold.* Every time we had run into each other since—once at a bar in the city, another time in the backyard of a house party, I think once on the street—I had been uncertain he would remember me at all.

I remembered, then, one long night we had spent together at the beginning. We had gone to a bar near my house and he had told me an involved story about how he was the best man for his friend's wedding happening that upcoming weekend, and how most of his responsibilities revolved around getting the good drugs. When we went back to my house, accordingly, he took out a pretty big bag of cocaine, and asked if I wanted some. "It's a Thursday night," I said, listing the reasons I shouldn't. "I have work tomorrow. It's already ten p.m." Of course I wanted some.

After, we realized there was a problem with the condom, and I became very angry—speedy and mean. I accused him of not wearing a condom at all. "Haley, I know you," he said, trying to get me to be calm. "You don't know me," I told him. "You know *a lot about me.*" The difference seemed important in that moment.

He walked me to the drugstore—by this point it must have been one a.m.—and walked me back home, sat with me on my stoop while I took the Plan B, smoked cigarettes until the drugs wore off and I could sleep. He was very decent about the whole thing. When I told this story to my friends we all agreed this was the only way a man in this situation could redeem himself.

The next day I had gone into work at eight a.m., as I always did, and left at one p.m., the way our office always did on Friday afternoons in the summer. I walked to a movie theater that was not close but was basically two straight lines away, a perfect L-shape of a walk, and crossed the street to stay in the shade as many times as there were blocks. I bought a sparkling water in a glass bottle. I sat in the balcony and sipped it while watching *Beau Travail* for the first time, feeling the sun in the desert on-screen like it was the air-conditioned cool in the dark room—a relief—and feeling the obsession between the men in the movie like it was in my body—an ache.

Teo came with me. They sat beside me and we didn't say one word until the lights came on.

T eo and I had met sideways, introduced at a friend's birthday party and then, months later, I was hired as an editor
at a publication where they worked as a writer. One afternoon they came to my cubicle because another coworker had told
them I would want to see their sweatshirt. It was screen-printed
with Gena Rowlands's upturned face, her eyes closed, a still from *A
Woman Under the Influence*. They were right, I told them. I absolutely
did want to see that sweatshirt.

On our lunch breaks we planned a union-organizing drive for
the office. We would go to this café that was small enough that we
could see everyone in there (no eavesdroppers), far enough away
that it didn't really make sense to walk there and back (no one
would look for us there), a little too expensive to be reasonable (too
decadent for two dirtbags). "I'm a socialist, because if capitalism
worked I'd be rich," Teo explained to me after we had ordered
scrambled eggs prepared with crème fraîche. "We're friends now,"
I said.

Back in our cubicles we would often pass afternoons between
meetings and deadlines listing movies to each other. Sometimes it
was just a report of what we'd watched; mostly they were assignments. They were movies that we needed to see to understand each
other. Teo, a critic and graduate of a film studies program, did

most of the assigning, and I took the responsibility very seriously. In my phone I kept a note called "Teo Movies" and beside every title there was a checkbox for me to mark off when I had seen it, when I was ready to tell them what I thought.

Most of the movies that we had both seen were divorce movies. Since my husband had moved out six months before, I had been watching and rewatching anything about breakups, endings, affairs—allegorical or realistic, romances and tragedies, I often described these evenings as though I was self-programming a divorced woman's film festival.

I knew what I was doing here. I even joked about it, suggesting to other people going through breakups that they redirect their hurt and sorrow into organizing their workplace. Into programming a film festival about their experience. Anywhere else but as something kept inside. The night before we were all laid off, I prepared myself for my last bargaining session to negotiate severance, and then I sat on the edge of my bed and wept—really wept—about everything for long enough until it all became a feeling as large and hopeless as nothing.

Being laid off did give us lots more time to go to the movies. If I hadn't seen a divorce movie that Teo recommended, watching it became an event. Once we went to a small movie theater that was showing what was then a rare print of *Possession*, the 1981 Andrzej Żuławski movie that Teo described as having cured their depression. This seemed unlikely until I watched it. Isabelle Adjani is so beautiful and so manic, her wardrobe entirely made of slightly different navy blue silk dresses. As a former ballet teacher, her movements are sadistic, every vein in her hand poised to draw blood and every step containing words she won't speak. Eventually we find out that she left her husband not for another man but for a hollowed-out flesh monster she fucks in a decrepit loft, while secret agents in brightly colored socks track the estranged couple under the over-cast West Berlin sky. Watching this movie cured my depression.

One night I watched *Take This Waltz*, a movie directed by Sarah Polley, filmed near the street I used to live on. The movie has that feeling of an afternoon when everyone is on their front porches, watching the neighborhood drama and everything that can hap-pen on a residential sidewalk. A marriage ends, a love affair begins. I worried the movie would make me too sad, as though recognizing where I once lived was too dangerous. Instead it made me feel the opposite of homesick. I was grateful for how far away I was from what I was seeing.

I was reminded of Stanley Cavell's interpretation of the class dy-namics in his chosen comedies of remarriage. He thought that wealth had to remain a given for at least one character: not because the working or middle class can't spend time inside their sadness, but because their days don't have the time to maintain the same dedicated interest in it. "This is why our films must on the whole take settings of unmistakable wealth," he wrote. "The people in them have the leisure to talk about human happiness, hence the time to deprive themselves of it unnecessarily." A movie or book about that sadness in between shifts would have so many smaller revelations, the single moments alone and unremarked on, but no less deeply felt. Like when I, on one workday, turned the corner in the hallway of my office kitchen and felt myself to be so completely grateful to be divorced. What would that have looked like? Like any other day, which it was.

The divorce stories want climax, resolution. Life wants nothing from you. This is not nothing in the sense of nonexistence; it is nothing in the sense that you are just another person in the world, your fortunes the result of your own judgments and your fates the result of your own interpretation, but there is no narrative that can compare to the recklessness of an ordinary day, of an average life lived. In considering the way life swallows up those moments as though they are like any other, I'm reminded of the way it feels to swim out into the ocean, past the crest of the waves before they roll in to shore. Once you are there the ocean considers the entirety of your existence the same as it considers everything else: as nothing in comparison to its own power. You cannot ask for a break, for solace, for recognition. You can barely ask to keep your head above water. There's only one choice. You can be in or out. Such forces tend to punish hesitation more harshly than anything else.

T eo and I became part of a large circle of friends, close at first because of circumstance and then increasingly closer over time—we had, we all frequently marveled, so much in common; and the ways we were different from each other felt fascinating, absorbing, impossible to understand and so even more necessary to figure out. We found ways to ask for the stories of our lives. We were really, really in love with dozens of people at once.

Our new collective of friends spent days and nights together, weekends full of that Saturday afternoon dehydration feeling—too much talking shit and laughing at our own jokes, the clutch at the front of our throats gone dry. Some of it went bad fast. There is no type of romance, friendship or otherwise, that can sustain that kind of sudden collision of intensity and proximity—the need to be safe with the risk of getting hurt. No one is ever, I started to believe, "just friends." That's the term for people we don't know very well yet. Real friendship is always what comes after the transitional stage on the way to becoming like something else. Like a sister. Like a family. Like a love.

We wanted so badly to be alike that we made ourselves so. I constantly felt like I was shoplifting someone else's experience, as though it were a drugstore nail polish slipped up my sleeve. Or it was playacting, pantomiming as though another person could be made into a scene from a movie or the motivation of a character in a novel. It all became a feeling that I was about to be caught with something that wasn't really mine.

"Being friends would be easier if it was just transactional," a woman I loved once said to me. "I do for you, you do for me, and that's that."

I agreed with her. It would be easier. I did not think that would make it any better. I was so angry with her in that moment.

That's not to say that any of those friendships really ended, or even that the hurt that ended up happening inflicted real damage. It's more that they threw into relief how desperately I needed to believe that ending my marriage meant I had chosen love, rather than whatever the opposite was. I wasn't ready to admit that one kind of relationship might start, but there was no way to truly divorce myself from whatever loves came before it. So much of my life is being in love with people I can't talk to anymore.

A lot of those friendships were made solid in similar moments. Later came a clear pattern. Within the group people would triangulate around an instance of pain: a breakup, mostly. The kind of grief that can feel uneasy or unearned in comparison to others. Many breakups can have the feeling of a life changed, but only some are given the gravity that lets us admit it. When it was a breakup—or even if it was just a moment of tension, a fight or a conflict or a bad feeling—many of us started behaving like we were some kind of emissary. In trying to be compassionate and good we would position ourselves between a person we liked and a person they loved. The intimacy between us was obvious. The spouses who looked at us and saw rivals were paranoid and they were right. Our closeness was capable of threatening theirs. Around this time a woman who worked as a therapist told me that people have to be careful not to fall in love with a person's pain just because that's where they need them the most.

Once, dangerously, my friends and I played a game of truth. We called it *shame types*. Everyone had to go around the table and admit what type of person they were ashamed to be consistently attracted to. Perhaps everyone answered honestly. Perhaps everyone played it the way I did: speaking an answer that sounded revealing and keeping in my head the one too real for words. Poets, I said when it was my turn. Everyone groaned with a pained, forgiving understanding. Other people's husbands, I thought.

Crucially, this game and our answers were not about who we actually got involved with—it was about who occupied our minds despite knowing better. I do not engage with other people's husbands except for, after a few too many strained and tense engagements, making more of an effort to ask them about their lives and work so that they are not annexed from the conversation I wanted to have with their wives. But I am always, always attracted to other people's husbands in the same way I can convince myself I want any style of interior design at someone else's house, or the dinner someone else ordered at a restaurant: if someone I trust already chose it.

My friend has done something wrong. A coworker of his tells me this one night as I'm closing our tab at the bar. My friend has done something *really* wrong to his wife, a woman he frequently and loudly proclaims to be in love with. I'm shocked; this was my friend's coworker's intention, I realize. He came here to break my heart.

I call my friend outside the bar and he doesn't pick up but texts that he's out, he'll call later. What would I say, I realize. If I ask him, he'll deny it. Besides, whether it's true isn't the point. I believe it the way I believe the temperature of the air when I stand outside. No one has to tell me what I feel.

I go home and stay up all night, and when the sun rises, I text Teo to come over. They bring cookie dough that they had put in their fridge the night before because a website told them that would make the cookies taste better, and I sit on my windowsill while they spoon cold dough onto a baking sheet.

"I'm too judgmental," I complain. "Too moral." We talk about how hurt I feel, about the hurt this man has spread around his coworkers, his friends, the people he is so quick to claim he loves. "When people try new ways of being in love, they want to think they're operating without expectations," Teo says. "Forgiveness for fucking up becomes their standard of morality."

We name the cookies after the actors from our latest favorite movie, Martin Scorsese's adaptation of Edith Wharton's novel about divorce, gossip, and forbidden romantic obsession, *The Age of Innocence*. I frequently thought of the scene when Daniel Day-Lewis begs Michelle Pfeiffer to trust that they can run away together; to abandon the conventions and taboos of Belle Époque New York and be free, even though he is married and she is divorced. Can't they go somewhere where that won't matter? "Where is that country?" Pfeiffer asks him, not entirely rhetorically. "Have you ever been there?" Teo is the one who told me that Scorsese considered *Innocence* the most violent movie he ever made—the violence that lovers do to themselves to deny happiness while still in its pursuit. When my new roommate comes into the kitchen after the oven dings, we offer him the cookie we named after Michelle Pfeiffer. "Oh, she's a great actress," he says, and leaves to eat it in his bedroom.

In August of the only year that I was married, my husband and I flew to the West Coast for a wedding. I was distracted; I didn't plan. Not understanding either Canadian geography or seasons, I had packed for what I considered to be August weather. I spent the entire time both cold and cursing myself for my missed opportunity to wear sweaters and jackets. The dress I brought was too big, and so were my shoes. But it was a beautiful wedding. I guess they all are. The bride's father, a carpenter, made the pews for the ceremony, and tables and chairs for the reception. The sun stayed on the water, and we traded blankets back and forth when the wind blew. At night we drank and cried too much. I had already said goodbye to these friends so many times before; when I had moved, when I came back to visit, and now when I would get back on a plane to fly to a different city than the one we grew up in together. "It doesn't get easier," one friend said through his tears. I held my hand on his cheek without wiping them away.

The day after the wedding I did some work, almost, while my husband and another friend rented a car. I had woken up in the morning with the idea that I wanted to go to nature. "I want to go talk to some mountains about my life," I said, and my husband had laughed, but I was only kind of joking. In the afternoon we started driving until the mountains started to look less like they were on the horizon and almost on the windshield. I pointed at the snow on the tips, and the cloud puffs above them with the water below, and the people walking by in appropriate hiking boots. I did not have appropriate hiking boots, but we walked anyway, carefully, not really talking but murmuring every so often. The trail we were on seemed to be coming to an end. The scene where it stopped was like a painting, two mountains overlapping behind a lake and under a blue sky, one small white cloud hovering between them.

Back in the city the season was more appropriate to what I expected and hated: airless, choking heat, sunlight that seemed to burn without warmth. Steam lifted off the sidewalk. The hours were slow and gone before I could count them. The feeling of August was as uncomfortable as the weather. Enough time had passed to know what this summer would be, but there was enough time to convince myself I might still be wrong. It was only four months before my husband would pack the suitcase and move out. In those nights, humid memories of the day kept me awake behind my closed eyes. I read the letters that writers I loved wrote to the people they loved, and circled the ones that felt important even if I couldn't say why. One I kept with me for a long time, waiting to understand how I knew what it meant—on August 12, 1971, Elizabeth Hardwick had written to Robert Lowell:

I have had a really fine summer, strange in many ways, in others exactly the same. In the afternoons the light drops suddenly, the day waits, and you feel a melancholy repetition, as though you were living moments before, maybe long ago by someone else.

In September she wrote to say that she had started divorce proceedings.

I n the year that I was married, I made friends with a woman as though she had always been there—her in my life felt more natural than the time before it. I admired a lot about her. She was younger and smarter: more education, more experience, much longer and far better hair. She also was engaged to a man she had fallen in love with when they were teenagers, but their relationship, she told me in one of our many long conversations about the time before we knew each other, was open. They dated other people. This was incredible, I told her, and privately thought this only confirmed what I felt about her manner of being in the world. She was sophisticated and brave, novel and classic. She had fun because she was fun. I invited her to my wedding, even though I didn't even know her at the time the original invites went out. Having her there felt exactly right.

One night, very soon after I was married, I hosted a small party at my house with a group of our friends, and we drank a lot of wine. Perched on the arm of my sofa, I leaned down to where she was sitting as she told a story about a new man she was seeing. "I want something like that," I whispered. "A boyfriend."

It wasn't the wine. I really did want something like that. I had never dated as an adult, and all my practice flirting was mostly contained to either my imagination or to developing an exceptionally friendly and sweetly persuasive demeanor in all my customer service jobs. Marriage could be, as everyone kept reminding me, anything we wanted. Why not this want?

I didn't mean something as literal as wanting the man she was dating, but when she suggested it I thought the same thing. Why not her want?

The man in question was another new addition to my friends. He had also moved recently, and people seemed very excited to have him live in our city. Everyone liked him, one mutual friend promised me, and then suggested that maybe he should rent the apartment I was about to leave. This was right after my husband and I decided to rent the slightly bigger unit just one floor up, and the small building of renters had an informal policy of offering our friends first dibs; we had only gotten that apartment because the previous tenants spoke to us before our shared landlord.

And so I had already met this man late one winter afternoon, when I showed him around my home. I could see why everyone liked him. He was calm, quiet, and nice. He looked right at me as I spoke, and I could tell he kept looking even after I looked away. Something about feeling that gaze made me nervous, jittery, shaken.

I saw him around regularly after that—at bars, on the street, once in line at the bank, as a guest at the housewarming party for the apartment he ended up renting instead—and never felt the same way again about the way he looked at me, so decided to forget it. When I heard this new man was dating my new friend, I thought that was nice. She liked him, too. These all seemed like good signs.

Her enthusiasm for matchmaking was well suited for my purposes: I was nervous about everything, but at least the person had been vetted by someone I trusted. With her blessing we started texting, an illicitness offset by the therapeutic languages I read about open relationships. I read *The Ethical Slut*. I learned so many new words. An entire vocabulary existed, and I believed that if you somehow used it correctly, any bad feeling could be made to evaporate. No one had to be jealous, I learned, and any hurt incurred could be healed. The rules that my husband and I had set for our open marriage were right, I thought at the time. They followed what I believed was the logic of what I had read. Disclosures and decorum, in equal measure—no lies, but also, no unnecessary details.

One night, after this man and I had both admitted that we wanted each other, I went to see him at a bar. I wore red lipstick. I leaned against the wall with the glass bottle I was drinking from in my hand, my winter coat held between my knees, worried I would let one or both drop from my grip when he leaned down to hear what I had said better. My husband was working out of town for the month, and we had agreed this would be the ideal time to try our new way of being married. This man could come to my place. He did. I was so nervous, and so certain of what would happen. I sat on my couch in a way that ended up being at odds with how he leaned toward me, his long legs crunched between the coffee table and the couch, and to compensate I found myself almost falling onto the floor, my arms holding on to the cushions like they could be an anchor, and I kind of laughed a little to acknowledge how very, very silly my position was.

"What's funny?" he asked, his mouth still on mine. His tone was very, very serious. Suddenly so was I.

"Nothing," I said.

Only later did I realize this matchmaking setup had been perhaps well-intentioned but not a good idea. The suspicion creeped in as I watched, like an outsider, five lives fold into each other with too much intensity too soon. My new friend and I; my husband and hers; our boyfriend. We delighted in our evolved approach as to who we were to each other. By the time I realized this was a bad idea it felt too late to stop. When I realized why it was a bad idea, it came with a clarity that felt worse for being so delayed. Almost better to have never known than to know so long after I needed to understand.

But I had wanted to date as an adult, and now I was. Now I knew how it felt to start wanting someone who wanted me in the same way; now I knew how quickly I would lose control of how much we wanted each other. How instead we would start to pick apart the knot that had twisted up between us both.

"He's not in love with you, is he?" my husband asked one morning as we had breakfast at our kitchen table.

I gave an exaggerated little spin in my chair, made a bunch of sputtering noises, as a tiny show of how ridiculous I found the question.

"OK," he said, probably embarrassed to witness such a performance. "You made your point."

This man wasn't in love with me. He wasn't in love with anybody, it seemed, though in conversation I would find out that the other women he saw wondered if that was a decision he made rather than a feeling he didn't have. His tendency was to lean toward the taken, and even when he saw women who were by any definition available, he preferred to speak about feeling second to their lives. One night at his house he talked about how it felt to be so intimately involved with this collection of women who returned home to their husbands in the morning.

In the moment I listened and said I was sorry.

Many months later I wondered what it meant that he viewed us as a collection.

There was a real desire at the beginning of this thing—lust that I now know was very true, and also too much for what I could handle then. That desire fit perfectly over what I was too afraid to admit: that I wanted a feeling more than I wanted anything else. That I wanted to be the kind of person who could chase lust without first negotiating the terms. That I wanted it so badly but somehow not badly enough to do anything smart or kind for everyone involved and leave my marriage. To leave my marriage and put down what had happened before that choice as my time of not knowing any better. To know when it was time to say goodbye, and to trust that we would have the chance to try again with other people. I did everything but that.

This man and I had been seeing each other about once a week for a few months when he offered to be my date for a work event we were both invited to. I packed a small purse with contact lens solution so that I could spend the night with him. I sat beside my friend, who'd packed her small purse with a flask we shared. Even though it was the kind of event with a dress code and caterers it was not the kind with an open bar. Somehow I forgot to bring a cell phone charger.

The whole night breathed of something wrong. My nervous feeling returned. We had been supposed to meet our friends first at a bar nearby, and he didn't show. Not wanting to waste my cell battery, I only texted once. Once he arrived he was distant. His jacket sleeves were sloping off his arms. He didn't want to talk. When the official part of the night ended he didn't want to come with me to the after-party, walking away when it was time to get in the cab.

At the bar I texted, again and again, until my phone died at the same rate as my dignity. The bartender offered to charge it for me. I considered the contact lens solution in my purse. I couldn't go home; not after telling my husband not to expect me. My friend with the flask had a couch, she reminded me gently. The feeling in my ribs had a hand on my throat and everyone could see it in my face. I smoked cigarettes outside and decided to wait five more minutes.

He did show up when I went back inside to collect my cell phone. I was standing in the corner, not wanting to join the small crowd of people desperate for the bartender's attention for such a silly reason as my phone. He saw me and approached.

"Are you having a good time?" he asked.

"No," I said.

He kissed me then in a way he never had in public. He hurt me in a way he never had in private. My arms bent behind my back at the wrong angle, my elbows held up like they didn't come attached to my shoulders. "We're leaving," he said.

In the car he took my ankle in his lap and ran his finger over and over the place where a silver strap was buckled. At his house he stopped me in the hallway. He handed me a glass or a bottle of whiskey, I don't remember which. "I don't want it," I told him. He made me drink it anyway. Most of it spilled on my dress. Wait, I said. Wait, wait, wait. We didn't wait. Afterward he said things he shouldn't have, either because I didn't believe he meant them or because I didn't want to admit how badly I wanted to hear him.

"You'll leave me," he said. "You'll go away and forget me."

"Yes," I said. "Yes. I'll leave. No. I won't forget."

ere's one part that doesn't fit in this story. On the way back from the morning after, when that man and I were walking toward my home, I got halfway down a block before realizing I was alone. I turned and he was stopped at a tree blooming with fragile purple and pink flowers. He was trying to get one off a branch and when he did he handed it to me. I took it the way I took everything he gave me in those months: grateful and embarrassed to want so badly what I knew I would have to give up.

To pick me a flower the morning after hurting me is not the part that doesn't fit. He was the kind of man who liked himself most for his contradictions, who believed there was meaning to be found in the distance between what kindness and cruelty he was capable of in the same weekend. "I think I would make a great character in a novel," he often joked in that way people do when their punch lines are the same as their wishes, and he behaved that way, living as though it was up to a reader to figure him out. No, to pick me a flower the morning after hurting me fits into who he was completely. To this day I will still sometimes remember something that he said he loved about me, like the way I would hide part of my face in his pillow some nights, and then be overcome with something that is part shame and part fear. He could remember that, too, anytime he wants. In his memory I am more his than I would have ever let myself be in his life, but not any less than I wanted to be. The part that doesn't fit about picking me a flower is how long I kept it pressed between the pages of a book. The part that doesn't fit is how long it took me to throw that dead flower away.

I guess now I've broken up with someone," I said to my husband as we walked home together one night a few weeks later. "I guess you have," he said.

IV

I was divorced on a cold day in the fall. The divorce lawyer was expensive. No matter how many times I explained it was a simple, uncontested divorce, she spoke like she expected us to produce some complication. Some asset we had forgotten. But we had our years and nothing else. "No property," she said when my husband and I went to her office for our first meeting, a question in her voice that seemed like a test. Her file folders were open, the long papers lit up under office bulbs. "No shared bank accounts?" We shook our heads. "No shared debts, no health insurance, no pets?" Nothing. Just time. Just years. My husband said, perhaps to make the conversation easier, "Just the Picasso." The divorce lawyer stopped and looked up, confused. "He's making a joke," I said. "We don't own any art." "Oh," she said. "I thought maybe you named your cat the Picasso."

I went home with forms to fill out, questions as mundane as they were invasive: How much was our rent when we lived together? How much did we spend on groceries? Who bought what, and why? The answers existed, but to think of them meant considering my marriage with more closeness than I had when we were together. The lawyer wanted to know about our life—all life, not just what we needed to keep ourselves alive. How much would I have remembered, these forms wanted to know, if we had stayed together? They wouldn't have been memories but routines; now it was over, and I was remembering a ritual I didn't have the rights to anymore. I remembered finding the last apartment we lived in together, and how happy I was that the previous occupants had built bookshelves that fit the walls perfectly. I remembered the afternoon I was home with a friend, talking on the couch, and my husband came home with groceries, and we both stopped to watch him put away the yogurt and apples, the frozen vegetables and the eggs; I remember him making dinner for us that night. I remember the window with the screen we could pop out to smoke. I felt myself realizing how wrong I had been, as a precocious child, telling my mother that divorce was the fastest way to get to know someone. I had meant that in moments of great grief or loss people tend to reveal their basest impulses, which is true enough; but in these forms my husband became a stranger and my marriage a ledger, a line of numbers I couldn't recognize as anything like a family. I don't remember, I told the lawyer. That's fine, she said. We just need a ballpark anyway.

Instead of filling out forms I watched the same movies, still acting as though I was studying how to be divorced. While *An Unmarried Woman* or *Heartburn* played on my laptop I would organize my closet, putting aside the majority of my wardrobe to sell. My wedding dress was long, white, silk, cut like a T-shirt—so simple—and sometimes I still tried it on to see if I could separate it from the wedding. But I knew the dress didn't fit me in any sense. I held off on deciding if I would keep or sell the wedding dress until that first meeting with the divorce lawyer, which I could not afford. I was out of money. After the movies stopped playing I would stay up all night every night googling *How bad before bankruptcy*.

One afternoon my husband came over to talk. *Fuck you*, he said halfway through, without explanation and with little connection to the conversation we were actually having. My face, I'm sure, looked the way it felt to hear him say that. *I'm sorry*, he said. I thought that maybe that was all he had come over to say.

The morning of our next meeting I carried most of my closet in my arms, watched as a consignment store buyer considered what I was offering. She took everything. I left with three hundred and eighty-nine dollars; the hour with the divorce lawyer would be four hundred dollars. I was relieved, though she gave my wedding dress a lower sticker price than my bomber jacket. Why did everything have to be such a metaphor all the time?

I took the cash to the meeting, which was our last. We signed as the lawyer timed us to see how quickly she could finish paperwork for a divorce this clean. We were done in twenty minutes; it would've been less if we hadn't paused to staple a few pages together. We had a full hour booked. "What else?" the lawyer asked. "What's next?"

I waited. I thought she would be the one to tell us.

December. Eleven months since my ex-husband had moved out. Our divorce had been filed in the courts closest to our new, separate addresses; he had insisted, saying he needed the closure. I wasn't sure what I needed and was skeptical about both concepts—paperwork is a fragile substitute for resolutions. I had said nothing then.

I unpacked a coat I hadn't sold, one I had bought many years earlier on impulse: I wanted to look the part, and while I couldn't remember what specific part I had been thinking of, I suspected it was some measure of picking what I thought my grandmother might pick if she wanted to look like she was playing the Katharine Hepburn role in a remarriage comedy. Camel and a wool-cashmere blend, the coat had a silk lining that had been ripped for almost as long as I'd owned it, snagged unluckily early and then ignored. When my husband left I took it to the tailor in a fit of productivity. I wanted to prove I could take care of something. I was so impressed with myself until the coat came back, repaired with such exacting perfection I couldn't even find the seam where the tear had been and the coins I had forgotten in the pocket were locked behind the lining. Every step I took I heard the coins—I ran my hands to where a dime and a nickel rested in a triangulated corner between the pocket and the hem, a jingling soundtrack that followed me everywhere. Like a joke Katharine Hepburn would make to Spencer Tracy. Every time I took the coat off I forgot about it. Every time I put it on I remembered this financial problem, far more adorable than any of my others, the coins clacking in time with my steps. I knew the solution but couldn't bring myself to purposely rip the lining and admit I had to start all over again.

Looking back I can see that I always knew what I would have done. I once knew that my husband was so completely mine, and so every choice that followed was only another version of that knowing. I would do it all again, which is not the same as saying I will. When I think about everything I can remember—as many memories as I can hold at once, and then the ones that come up later, surfacing when I least expect them—I know I would do it all exactly the same, with all the same answers. I would say yes, say more, say never, say no.

E arly December wasn't as cold as it seemed like it should be. I still wore the coat with the coins but didn't need a scarf, or some days even a sweater underneath. There was a coffee shop slightly too far away from my house for me to visit as often as I did, but I still preferred it to anything closer. It had a deep, bright blue door, and a large backyard; the people who worked there were, I flattered myself thinking, like me—friendly but quiet. We would speak a little, most of the conversation between us smiles instead of words.

On some Sunday mornings, I would wake up earlier than I wanted to, just to be there before it was busy. They offered a size of coffee that was too large to be reasonable, which I loved. It was the first Sunday of December when I ordered that coffee and took it to the backyard, pulled the coat around me, and as if I had planned it all along, I dialed my mother's number.

Being away from home had meant I hadn't had to think about what my family did or didn't know about my life. We were most accustomed to talking about the facts of our days, telling stories of what we had done or seen. Even if it was an omission or a deflection, not telling my parents about my divorce in that first year didn't feel like a trial, or even a deliberate choice. I just didn't want to, and I found I didn't have to. I took the easy way out for as long as I could.

I really didn't know how my mother would respond. I really didn't know what I hoped she would say. I didn't feel I could handle too many questions, and I also worried that I would agree with an expression of my worst fear. If she asked how it could be that my marriage was over so soon; how I could have divorced so young; how I could have kept this from her for almost a year; I would have no satisfactory answers. I didn't know either. I didn't think it was right either.

I told her the truth when she picked up: I was calling to tell her my husband and I had separated. She didn't seem surprised, and that also didn't seem strange at the moment. Maybe I had been more obvious than I thought. She asked only a few questions, and I told her what I knew I could answer. It wasn't a relief exactly; more like I was finally accepting something that had already happened. Maybe not wanting to tell the people who mattered most was about giving my husband and me one last secret. One last thing we would know about who we were to each other before everyone else decided they knew who we were.

I spent Christmas alone in the city. A movie theater uptown was showing a melodrama series, and Teo insisted I see the Max Ophüls 1948 film *Letter from an Unknown Woman*. They described it as the greatest romance that is almost certainly a story of a stalker and her obsession, and assured me this detail was obscured into irrelevance, and I would see for myself that both actors were so hot it seemed cute.

Letter from an Unknown Woman is a story about love that can only exist beside an object of affection—love that takes shape around what's possible, wanting more than what you have while lacking the bravery to live without it. The same month I saw the film for the first time, the critic Molly Haskell published a brutal essay about it, on the topic of soulmates and other betrayals of repetition: "The philanderer is like the serial killer, compelled to repeat his pattern," she said. "The woman, too, shares the pathology of the compulsive criminal, her sacred love the equivalent of his sacred vice, both thrill to the sense of superiority it gives them over ordinary unsuspecting mortals."

The theater was full of women in fur coats sitting in groups of two and three—most of them in their sixties or older—and I sat in one of the few remaining seats available by the front of the screen, all that was left twenty minutes before the movie even started. The audience for *Unknown Woman* was just like the audience at *Waiting to Exhale*—they knew every line by heart. Mine broke, again and again, thinking about the superiority and the stupidity of that sacred self-righteousness Haskell described. She ends her essay by warning how this form of romance will wreck any life it enters. "How better to own your passion, keep it pure and undefiled, and thus in line with image of self as selfless love than unrequited love?!" she writes, exclamation her own. The untried and the untested, to those lost in their own obsessions, at least mimic the transcendent. Sometimes I look at a couple and I think I can see what it was they thought they wanted—can see so clearly that to each other they represent great risk or great reward, even when the compromises they've made are just as transparent.

M y grandmother had a long run of bad years, her health failing in different ways. She got quieter as her hearing got worse. I went to visit her when she moved into a home for seniors, the contents of her former bathroom mirror lined up on the ledge of her new window: pink bottles of creams, boxes of silver hair clips. One conversation I taped, wanting to have the sound of her voice saved. (Later I realized that the voice I wanted saved was the one I remembered from when I was a teenager at her dinner table, but I would have never thought of that then.) We talked about her divorces, a phrase just as glamorous as her husbands. In the recording I can hear the beeps of a machine in the next room; I can hear the workers walking by in their Crocs. My grandmother gestured to a cup by her bed, where she kept a pencil for the crosswords in the newspapers my mother brought her. *You make a mistake, you rub it out*, she said, pointing to the erasers.

Did you think your marriage was a mistake? I asked.

She shrugged in her way—my way now—smiling small, as though she couldn't help but admit the answer was yes, her ear dipping toward her right shoulder.

There's no reason why people should stay together when they're not happy together. We went through it, she said, and made a circle with her arm to show the "we" included my mother and me with herself. *We know what it's like. It's no fun. But it has to be done in most cases.*

My mother asked her if she was relieved when she got divorced.

Oh my god, yes.

Say more! we laughed. *Tell us more.*

I was so relieved. I couldn't wait for it to be over. And relief is more than just a word—it was a whole feeling. I should have done it years before, and not waited; there was always a reason to wait. A kid's birthday, you know. Until it comes to you and it's almost too late.

I explained to her the concept of divorce parties—celebrations after a divorce is finalized.

I didn't do that. But I did celebrate for myself. I changed my name, I went right to work. I succeeded at work. I had one job after another, and they were all good, and I did well. But I wouldn't recommend working. I recommend divorce highly.

When I left that last time, I said, "I'll see you soon, OK?" As though it was a question to ask; as though she could confirm I would. "I hope so," she said.

My mother called me early one morning a few weeks later, to tell me my grandmother had died in the night. Like the funerals I remembered as a child, there was no time to do anything but react— I had to return to my home city, to the funeral home that performed Jewish services, where the furniture had not changed in either my lifetime or my parents' lifetimes. *This looks exactly the same as when our paternal grandfather died,* my sisters and I whispered to each other as we walked in. He had died fifteen years earlier. "This looks exactly the same as when my father died," my mother whispered to us as we sat in that back room for families. Her father had died over forty years ago.

Over the years my grandmother's apartment still hadn't changed much. The fridge was still covered in the same baby photos, a love letter I had written her when I was probably six or seven after learning what it meant to be anonymous: "Dear Annette, I love you. Love, your secret admirer," it read in my elementary school best cursive, every letter in each word connected by a pencil swoop. The guest bedroom where my sister and I had slept, the room where she kept her computer and most of her books, covered in the same combination of textiles: quilts and pillows and scarves. In her bedroom I went through the drawers the way I used to, not really sure why— even if I found something, I wouldn't be able to ask her what it meant. I tried to remember the stories she told at dinner. I worried that my memories had no sound, or rather no words. I could see but not hear my grandmother talking.

In one drawer my sisters and I found the photos of my father she had stored after my parents' divorce. Tactful, we agreed, to put them away rather than throw them out.

Before and after my wedding I sometimes thought about how my mother had told me that she was with my grandmother in the moments before she married her second husband. They divorced when I was still a baby. I don't remember him at all; my grandmother did not talk about him. My mother remembers my grandmother, hesitant, before her wedding ceremony. "I don't think I should do this," she said. She did it anyway. Now I sometimes wonder what she was thinking about. I know she didn't want to get married, but I wonder if it was because she was thinking of her past or her future.

I had known, for many years, a man who was what I considered a serious writer. Very serious books. Very solemn essays. We had lots of friends in common; through several strange coincidences, he later became friendly with my aunt. In the months when I didn't want to say I was divorced he had—either by accident or in carelessness—told her that it looked like I had left my husband, and my aunt told my mother. That was why she hadn't been surprised when I told her.

I found out a long time after, when my grandmother was sick and this man began to ask, occasionally but without much follow-through, if I was interested in dating him. I told my mother. When she told me he was the one who was responsible for her knowing about my divorce I was angry; I thought it spoke to the reasons I was already slow to trust him. "Maybe it was an accident?" my mother offered, trying to encourage me to forgive him before I had even asked for an apology. I didn't want to see his way of watching as something that had its own meaning, that maybe he was paying too close attention and hadn't understood how easily he could overstep. "Even so," I said.

We were quiet again. "I don't think he takes me very seriously," I said, looking for more excuses. "Also, it seems like he mostly prefers to date women who are younger than me." "Hm," my mother said. "Does that make you feel bad about yourself?" "*No*," I said. "It makes me feel bad about . . . himself."

When we still had Shabbat dinners we often gossiped about the main characters of our family—always wives, rarely husbands. Sometimes my sisters and I asked our mother and aunt for more stories about my grandmother and her marriage. One dinner table classic went like this: My grandfather had promised my grandmother he was no longer seeing another woman, but they lived in a small neighborhood within a big city. My grandmother quickly found out this was a lie. Worse, she found out that he had arranged for his girlfriend to go with him on a business trip. My grandmother's best friend, a wonderful woman who had died when I was still a teenager and was, I thought, the true love of my grandmother's life, had convinced her to leave her teenage daughters for the weekend and fly to the hotel where this conference was happening. She told her to knock on my grandfather's door to confront him. My grandmother did exactly this.

"Then what happened?" my sisters and I asked.

"Your grandmother's friend flew home with the other woman, and your grandmother stayed until the conference was over and flew home with your grandfather."

"Wasn't that flight home with the girlfriend so awkward?"

"No," my mother said. "Well, maybe a little. They already knew each other from the Jewish community center."

Once the facts as we knew them had been discussed, we turned to speculating. This intervention only lasted a few years before my grandparents divorced. My mother said this story was how she became convinced that my grandmother never really wanted to be divorced. Why would she fly to confront him unless she didn't plan to divorce him?

"Did she not want to get divorced?" I asked. "Or did she think she couldn't not be married?"

Nobody is sure how to answer this.

The friends I stayed with throughout my grandmother's shiva are the ones I once helped make cupcakes on a hot day. They have an actual family home now, not just the feeling of one: a baby, a cat, a dog, a small backyard that opens up into a large park, a basement with a bed that's always made for me, and a bathroom I share with the cat.

In between visits to my grandmother's apartment, I sprawled on the floor with their baby. He was surprisingly strong, and constantly hurting the cat. *Gently, gently,* we told him, miming the petting we wanted him to practice. My friend ended up prying the baby's tight fists from the cat's fur while the cat bit both of them. The baby cried. *Well, that's what he'll do when you hurt him,* she said. She showed again how she pets: her long fingers are so soft and her motions so smooth. Her baby lost interest in the animal and crawled to his baby-size piano. When it was time for his dinner I carried him to the high chair. My friend put tiny bushy stalks of cut broccoli onto his tray. He picked one up by the stem and held it tightly in his fist, considering its bushy head, and softly, softly stroked the broccoli, the way we wished he would pet the cat.

I was married until I was divorced. In the years after, I often found myself away from home. I traveled for work more than I ever had; I visited friends to meet their babies, to give speeches at their weddings; I watched empty houses and watered plants. Once I went to Paris for a brief job. When I landed I dropped my bags, tried to go for dinner, but the place I chose wasn't serving food at that time. The bartender was a tall man who kept his cigarettes behind his ear, and his cat walked up and down the bar, pausing to poke her nose in my glass. I asked him the cat's name. "Do you know what *rillettes* means?" he asked. I did, but I wanted him to explain it, and why he had named his cat after pâté. When I went to pay, I realized I had left my wallet in one of my other bags. "I'm so, so sorry," I told him. "I'll be back in twenty minutes." He said *d'accord* with a smile like he knew he would never see me again. When I came back in twenty minutes his smile was shocked. The cigarette that had been behind his ear was lit in his hand, and I thought he was going to drop it when I held out my cash. I could have left and never come back, it's true. The thought even occurred to me. But what I could do and will do are almost never the same.

He made me some french fries, the only food available on the menu in the early evening, and I accepted it even as I berated myself for settling. I should have double-checked the menu and the hours. I should have said *Merci, de rien,* and then left to find another bistro. Instead I had french fries and Diet Coke for dinner and thought of how my grandmother would have been so disappointed in me. While I was away I often thought of my grandmother, who had traveled extensively throughout her marriages. I bought magnets at every museum I visited to make my fridge look like hers; not to re-create exactly, but certainly in spirit. She had photo albums full of moments I envied and kept me in awe of her life before I existed: like the photos of her sitting on top of a camel, or sitting in front of the Louvre with a silk scarf around her neck, and then suddenly, on one page, a photo of Diana Ross in a striped T-shirt brushing her hair away from her face. "Why do you have a photo of Diana Ross in here?" my sisters and I asked her the first time we saw it. My grandmother shrugged. They had been eating at the same restaurant and she had simply asked if she could take Diana Ross's photo and Diana Ross said yes.

When I looked around the Parisian restaurant, I saw there were two other girls sitting across the room beside the open window. They were smoking and looking at their phones, periodically putting their cigarettes in the ashtray and absentmindedly eating their way through the same shallow plate of fries, their straws bobbing in glass Diet Coke bottles. I felt better. Maybe I was wrong about what my grandmother would or wouldn't have done on an exhausted first night of a trip. Maybe she also was sometimes tired enough to consider skipping the trip to the museum she had basically come to a city just to see, and then when she got there, dragged her shoes along the marble halls, sore and irritable and unmoved by the glamours of history. Still, this goes against what I hold on to as her character. I remember her not just as virtuous but with the toughness that makes virtue—the will to walk long distances even when tired, to clean even the most annoying corners, to take care with her cashmere, to hold out for the better bistro.

I was only back home for a few weeks before it was time to go to more weddings, another plane and then a train. I passed the ugly corners of city limits, the gray poles and barbed wire of power grids and train tracks. I could just barely make out a deer galloping through a field as the window went by. These weddings were mostly without ceremony, natural and improvised. At some I was being introduced to the groom for the first time; at others it was an entire room of people I had known for decades. There was one person I knew would be at two weddings scheduled for two consecutive weekends, and we agreed to wear the same outfits without acknowledging the repetition. When I showed up at the second wedding she was wearing a new dress.

"Hey," I said, "what the fuck?"

She shrugged. "I went shopping."

Any wedding has its own tense sensation. If it is a room of single people, it is the sexual tension of unknowing (*could you?*). If it is a room of coupled people, it is the sexual tension of obligation (*you should*). A wedding is that rare setting where both are equal and crossed—a reminder that even after making what is, presumably, the biggest commitment of your relationship, everything that follows will still have to feel like a decision to make rather than a choice to live. The single adults congregate in corners, ignoring each other until their third drinks. The couples spread out, making small talk, until the music starts, and then they find each other.

Sometimes my ex-husband was also invited and I would spend hours in advance of the event imagining how to prepare myself, how to avoid feeling what I knew I would feel when I saw him. In an ideal situation, I explained to a friend, I would simply walk up and say hello, introduce myself to his girlfriend, and then say that I was on my way to the bar and did they need anything? When they politely declined, I would make sure to put my entire foot down before walking away so I wouldn't stumble on my exit.

I remember February of the only year we were married. Sixteen of our closest friends organized a trip, and because it was only two months after they planned our wedding, they agreed to treat it as though it was our honeymoon. At night we played drinking games and in the morning we took care of our hangovers like they were precious, passing around glasses of ice water and plates of buttered toast at the breakfast table, placing T-shirts over our eyes and hats over our heads as we lay down to rest by the water. In the afternoon we swam, dried off while reading novels in the sand, showered, and napped, so we could repeat it all over again. This was, to this day, one of the only true vacations I've ever taken, and it had been an immense amount of stress to find a trip that could accommodate the different budgets and schedules of such a large group of friends. Still, we all agreed it was worth it. Who knew what might happen in the next few years? My husband and I were planning to move, our other friends were starting to plan for babies; we might never be this free again.

I had been anxious about this vacation for a lot of reasons, worried about being away from work and unsure how I would do in a resort-style environment, but once again I was able to relax and trust that my friends knew best. They had an endless supply of drinking games for after dark, conversations for the beach; we traded the books we had brought and sometimes read them aloud to each other. (One of the only videos still on my phone is of one of our most wholesome friends, Mitch, blushing as we laugh at his recitation of someone's airport copy of *Fifty Shades of Grey*. He always seems to be a little embarrassed both by the book and to be caught laughing.)

On one of the few cloudy days, we signed up to go on a day trip to a nearby city. It was cold but beautiful. We visited churches and landmarks. There's a picture of us from that trip that I remember well. We were in the city, looking at the architecture. I am holding on to my husband tight in the cold air, my back to the camera and his arms around me.

Later we stopped in a hotel to change into our outfits for dinner and dancing. The girls traded curling irons for their hair, the boys passed around an iron for their shirts. We ate, we danced, we got drunk. We smoked. I smoked too much, allowing myself a vacation's idea of moderation. My husband drank too much. We took a bus back to our hotel. I coughed and coughed and coughed. He kept putting his hands on my thighs and I kept pushing them away, trying to cough out a *stop*. I was, I thought, choking. I was wearing the only dress I'd brought, a slip dress with lace trim, and my husband's hands were on my thighs, under the skirt, then on my neck, my chest. I couldn't talk to tell him to stop. I pushed him off.

Back at the hotel I sat on the bed watching him pace. The walls were so thin we could hear it when a friend next door dropped a toothbrush. He was angry; we were angry at each other—now that I could breathe, I still didn't want him to touch me. *But you're my wife*, he said. Everything else was too ugly to be remembered. Many of the details are lost to me, now that I have spent so much time trying not to think of it. Hopefully the same is true of the friends on the other side of the thin wall. When we apologized to each other we did so sincerely, honestly, completely. I still know that I'll never forget it. It marks a before and after that I wish didn't exist. Only eight weeks into our marriage, I felt what he meant. He was owed something. I didn't want him to have it.

In both memories, of the photograph and of that night, I feel myself looking at the back of my head, held still in air colder than I would have expected. In the photo I can't see my face but somehow I can see something important: how young I'd been.

I could never make sense of what had happened to me during my first real breakup after my divorce. When I had ended things with Dylan I had been, in every respect, broken, and that had felt proof that it must be me who couldn't make love work, me who had failed my marriage. How could I be falling apart over a man I'd only known for a few months? When my husband had moved out I cried lots, but I cried while functioning. I worked, slept, ate, walked around with friends. In the weeks after Dylan, I passed out at my office and was placed on an emergency sick leave. I couldn't concentrate on anything and so I couldn't think; it was like my brain and my body could only be on at separate intervals, and if I tried to use both I would collapse. Friends came over with soup and pressed their extra Ativans into my palm, begging me to sleep or eat, and I would consider myself to be explaining something as I rambled without a point or logic beyond begging that they not confuse this with my feelings about my divorce. This sadness, I tried to say, was not about my marriage, was not a sideways form of expressing a grief I wasn't yet ready to admit. *I know what everyone is thinking*, I would tell them. *I know what people are going to say but they're wrong, they're wrong. OK*, they would say.

Of course it was about my marriage. Of course it was about Dylan. Of course it was both. Maybe I worried they wouldn't take me seriously, or that I couldn't risk being misunderstood. Maybe I sensed that the simplest explanation of pain could offer something straightforward enough to be shared—the very opposite of how it feels to explain a marriage on the verge. Nothing seemed ordinary after my divorce because nothing could be. The institution hadn't defined my feelings, but it had changed the shape of them in a way I couldn't have predicted and probably would never recover from. Now I knew that whatever still might happen in my life and with whoever I might meet I wouldn't settle for anything less. I didn't know yet that one ending might happen first, but no ending is ever really over.

As a teenager, I remember seeing my husband walk into the hallway where everyone hung out before classes started, looking up as he shuffled in for the punch line to some joke I hadn't heard, and then looking away to go back to a book. Later he told me he had seen me looking and felt embarrassed, unsure if I was judging him or thought he was too silly. I really hadn't thought either. I had just seen it and thought nothing. In the only class we had together, he told me about how at the very beginning of the year we were placed in a group together and he had eavesdropped on my conversation with a friend about a movie we had both watched over the weekend. She had liked it, I hadn't. "I agreed with you," he said. I didn't remember the conversation but the opinions he recounted did sound like mine.

So I had been watched exactly the way I had wanted to be, like a character in a book—without my knowing but without embarrassing myself, by someone who cared what I thought as well as liked hearing what I had to say. I was too lucky, I thought, too lucky and so inevitably cursed. No one had ever wanted me before and the logic followed, I thought, that no one ever would again. Well, so what? This was all I wanted—this boy who already seemed way more like an adult than I was, solid and reliable and believing in a future I doubted would ever come for me. He got good grades, had fun with his friends, participated in extracurricular activities, and got his driver's license. He wanted to be a filmmaker and so he made films. He talked about going to Los Angeles. "Maybe I could come with you," I said.

"Maybe . . ." he said, and so I didn't mention it again, but thought about little apartment complexes with palm trees bookending the driveway, getting a job as a makeup artist. Everyone had seemed to suggest that being with someone who wanted to be with you would result in some sort of life-altering change, some feeling of elation or belonging, and they were right. Now that he was there I could think about a future: his. I wanted to go into what was next if it meant I could do it with him.

I became as proud of saying *my divorce* as I had once been of saying *my husband.* I felt ownership of my status; it was mine to obsess over, in all its instances and expressions. Being divorced made me, I was told again and again, different. I was part of a small scene that felt astoundingly large, and there were so few of us within who could say *my divorce* and mean it. That seemed important. There was a significance to it that was appropriate, and manageable. It was a fact about who I had been before these people knew me that was, according to them, worthy of notice. In this form being divorced was only ever a party trick, nothing more.

The longer I clung to it the more territorial I became, marking a status out of what mostly felt—as far as I would allow myself to feel it—like an accident. I had said *my husband* in this exact same way: making something mine to avoid asking whether I had wanted it, or whether I was capable of admitting I had chosen it.

To bury myself in the significance of being divorced meant I cataloged facts and details that I believed to be, in the moment of gathering, precious. Most of them were useless. People learned to bring me information and I loved that, though I was never quite sure what to do with it. I remember one of these exchanges in particular. A friend told me of learning the difference between what are called "capstone" and "cornerstone" marriages, and the way these categories often sorted themselves between certain socio-economic lines. People like her, who studied and then worked in rigorous, stressful professional fields, were more likely to have the cornerstone marriage: they married relatively early in life, as a way of turning a corner, so to speak, into adulthood. By choosing their spouse, they could consider themselves free to focus on the demands of their work. People like me, who had chosen careers with less of a linear path to achievement, were more likely to have the capstone marriage. They typically married a little later in life, after they felt that they had accomplished what they needed—the cap marking the end of a transitional, searching phase of adulthood.

These experiences were foreign to me, but I recognized the truth of their patterns. Such knowledge must matter, if not to me then at least just somewhere hovering around me.

Couples keep their secrets. Divorcés have no such commitments. After a marriage ends there is sometimes what feels like a flood of information: there is no bottom to what a recently divorced person can remember and then put into words. Of course, the fact that they can speak freely doesn't mean that they do, or that what they say means more than what they keep to themselves. They have every reason to share a partial or incomplete string of sentences. They could be speaking to assuage their own guilt, or because they need someone else to also condemn their former partner.

Or maybe: divorcés keep their secrets. Couples have no such commitments. In a marriage, spouses have to live with the presumption of intimacy. They are very quick to find their own ways to stay distant. The rush of disclosures on a rare night apart makes for a thrilling, imbalanced trust—now someone else, some chosen third, knows something that a spouse doesn't.

Of course, the fact that they can speak freely doesn't mean that they do, or that what they say means more than what they keep to themselves. *The only person we can keep a secret from is ourselves.* Sharing too much is an excellent substitute for thinking enough. When we are glib about marriage it feels like being sacrilegious, in a good way. When we are the same about divorce there is an air of profanity, of vulgarity. Both sides hurt. They hurt so good.

When I did finally understand that there are two sides to every story, it required letting go of my previous understanding, which is that very basic version fit for kids and other precious idiots. It is not a maxim designed to teach you that no one is wholly right or wrong. It is only that no one ever believes themselves to be entirely one or the other. The side of the story that they tell depends on their ability to consider whether the same is true of other people. Whether you are married or divorced, single or committed, in love or brokenhearted—that, too, is just a list of qualities that can never be the sum total of what a person is. We are always capable of being more than one.

This was one of those epiphanies that are basically meaningless, much like a big thought one has right before falling asleep. If it was so profound, why was it so hard to remember the next morning?

Adrienne Rich wrote in *Of Woman Born*, her book about motherhood, that she told herself she wanted to write about being a mother because it was an important idea still unexplored in feminist theory. That was true, and also not. The truth was, she admitted, that the subject chose her.

I thought I chose divorce as a subject because it was necessary, by which I meant there was still something unseen and unsaid about what was everywhere. I thought I chose divorce because of circumstances—my grandmother, my mother, my marriage. I had not chosen to inherit or live those stories of separation, but I had, and so the resulting calculations suggest: Shouldn't I make use of them somehow? I took many small, precious objects that had belonged to my grandmother after she died, but the only one I keep on me everywhere I go, safe in a small zipped pouch, is her gold seashell measuring tape.

Divorce was the subject that chose me. Right inside it was everything I wanted and feared the most: decisions and choices, isolation and entrapment, loneliness and romance. The terror of wondering what story my life would be was a perfect distraction from wondering why life needed to be a story.

Once my mother asked my sisters and me if her career had influenced the way we thought about marriage. No, we told her, which was true. Maybe we have a more practical understanding of divorce. Like everyone else, we know it in our own way.

There is no typical divorce, no one narrative recognizable to the millions and millions of people who know better, yet marry anyway, for their own reasons—for love, for security, as a calculated reaction or as a leap of faith. It is not that divorce reveals a more elemental aspect to a person's character—although it certainly can—but that it is the only way to find out who we are in those moments of pain, loss, and shame that come after standing up in front of the people you trust and love the most, only to say later that you hadn't known what you were doing.

When I remember my wedding I remember my dress, my shoes, my friends putting up the decorations, and our mothers, who we love, crying and holding hands as my husband and I put on our rings. I know that my marriage and my divorce and the fact that no-fault divorce exists at all do not answer the questions worth asking: Who did you choose, and who chose you? Who did you leave, and who left you? To be wanted is one thing, and to be left is another. The gravity in either direction is stunning, if you think about it for long enough. And then there's the only question that matters: *But what happened after?* The answer is that it is still happening.

ACKNOWLEDGMENTS

The first person to know that I was writing a book, long before I did, was Dayna Tortorici. The friend who always knew what I needed—whether it was a word or a hand or a walk or a meal or a book or a song or to sit in silence beside each other—and still knows, to this day, is Dayna Tortorici. Thank you for being my forever editor and the very best friend.

Thank you to Marya Spence, for representing me and my writing with the intelligence, compassion, and fierceness that has made her such a formidable literary agent; I am a luckier writer for working with her. Thank you to Allison Lorentzen, who instantly made me feel like my writing could be a book and always understood what I hoped my book would be. Thank you to Haley Cullingham and Jared Bland, for being such wonderful and enduring presences in my career and my life. Thank you to Clare Mao, Mackenzie Williams, and Camille LeBlanc, for all your support before, after, and during the process of making this book.

The second person to know that I was writing a book was Susan Orlean. In her capacity as the Rogers Communication Chair for the literary journalism program at the Banff Centre for Arts and Creativity, I learned and grew so much; just being in her presence, let alone participating in her workshops, was a master class in literary nonfiction, and her handwritten notes on the earliest version of *No Fault* is one of my most priceless possessions. Thank you, Susan.

Thank you to the Banff Centre for Arts and Creativity for supporting this book by accepting me into the 2018 literary journalism program, where I was able to concentrate on my writing with all the luxuries of space and time provided for me. Thank you to Ainslee Beer, Samantha Culp, Tim Falconer, Philip Gourevitch, Kathleen McLaughlin, Grant Munroe, Devon Murphy, Meghan Power, Jodi Rave Spotted Bear, Katie Sanders, Carol Shaben, and Lawrence Wright. A special thank you to Linda Besner and Matthew J. Trafford, for all our conversations about work and writing but mostly all our conversations about everything.

Meeting Colleen Kinder when she visited Banff changed my life, as I've told her every opportunity I can. Thank you, Colleen, for that moment in time, and everything since.

Thank you to the Robert B. Silvers Foundation for their invaluable support of *No Fault* with their grants for works in progress. I will always be grateful that such a generous program for writers exists and that I was lucky enough to benefit from it in 2020.

A version of my writing on Phyllis Rose and *Parallel Lives: Five Victorian Marriages* first appeared in *The New York Times Magazine*, while a version of my writing on Jessie Bernard and *The Future of Marriage* first appeared in *Topic*. I wrote about Deborah Levy's memoir trilogy for *n+1*, and I wrote about *The Continuing Story of Carel and Ferd* on an assignment for *Affidavit*. A short anecdote in this book about visiting my divorce lawyer also appeared in an essay for *The Baffler*, and the paragraph about the first August I was married appeared in my essay "Against August" for *The Paris Review*. Thank

ACKNOWLEDGMENTS

you to the excellent editors I worked with: Nitsuh Abebe, Madeline Leung Coleman, Kaitlin Phillips, Bidi Choudhury, Sophie Haigney, and the editorial board of *n+1*. Thank you, as well, to Max Nelson at *The New York Review of Books* and Jordan Larson at *New York* magazine. Thank you to Lucy McKeon, for being the reader I needed right in the middle of writing. Thank you to Sean Lavery, for being both the most professionally thorough and emotionally reassuring fact-checker I could have ever hoped for. Thank you to Rebecca Storm, for letting us use your beautiful painting on the cover. Thank you to Janique Vigier, my dream partner in all things related to publishing a book.

Jia Tolentino and Emma Healey read early versions of my manuscripts, and, as first readers and friends, have been a constant source of inspiration, kindness, and joy in my life. Thank you, both.

Thank you to Tavi Gevinson, Sophie Mackintosh, Charlotte Shane, and Lynne Tillman, for being writers I trust and admire so much. Your support sustained me through to the very end of writing and the beginning of letting the book go into the world, and I'll always remember that.

Thank you to Teo Bugbee, for making everywhere we are together feel like home. Thank you to Durga Chew-Bose, for being my forever inspiration as a reader, writer, editor, and, above all else, the woman I'm so lucky to call my friend. Thank you to Maria Dimitrova, for starting our conversation, which has lasted every day since and still will never run out of words. Thank you to Anna Fitzpatrick, for always having a key to wherever I had a door. Thank you to Emma Janaskie, for your style and standards. Thank you to Jazmine Hughes, the love of my life. Thank you to Naomi Skwarna, for the beauty you have and the beauty you give in equal measure. Thank you to Doreen St. Félix, for being my constant source of brilliance in all types of illumination.

So much support for the writing of this book came from two families in particular, and I'm very thankful for the love and friendships they've given me in the many years we've known each other. Thank you to Adam, Laura, Ori, River Rose, and Wavy Goldhopf for always having a room for me in your home. Thank you to Laura Fisher, Ali Shamas Qadeer, and Rosie and Lila Fisher Qadeer for always having a place for me at Friday night dinner.

Thank you to Zoe Badley, Alex Balk, Sarah-Joyce Battersby, Adam Bayard, Brian Benson, Liz Bertorelli, Rachael Bridge, Amy Bond, Mitch Boughs, Stephanie Brownlow, Matt Buchanan, Lisa Budd, Marian Bull, Emma Carmichael, Clio Chang, Hazel Cills, K. Austin Collins, Andrew Daley, Allison P. Davis, Sam Donsky, Kate Dries, Michael Ellis, Robin Ennis, Pedram Eynolhagh, Tess Fraad-Wolff, Jackson Fratesi, John Furnish, Dylan Going, Sarah Hagi, Rachel Handler, David Hill, Clover Hope, Erika Lee Houle, Matthew Judd, Kim Keitner, Jesse Noah Klein, Kate Knibbs, Danielle LaSusa, Jo Livingstone, Roderick Mackay, Merry Maclellan, Katie McDonough, Katie McMillan, Megan McRobert, Amber Meadow Adams, Michael Mlotek, Nimarta Narang, Adam Nayman, Gabby Noone, Puja Patel, Lola Pellegrino, John Pichette, Nadine Rashad, Britt Rawlinson, Ying Reinhardt, Steve Saunders, Thora Siemsen, Estelle Tang, Will Tanner, Anna Vodicka, Simon Vozick-Levinson, Olivia Whittick, Darcie Wilder, Romany Williams, and Gaby Wilson.

Thank you to Aviva, who is my little princess, and the only royalty I recognize. Thank you to my sisters (seestras), Erin and Jackie, for being the very best people I know, and the ones I look up to the most. Thank you to my mother, Risa, for taking me to the library as often as I wanted and letting me take out as many books as I could carry. You filled our home with books, for pleasure and for work, and you showed me how to live a life made of independence, strength, curiosity, attention, and very loud laughter.

I wish my grandmother Annette was here so that I could tell her all the ways I keep her with me, but writing her into these pages has been, at least, one way of expressing that feeling. Thank you for reading about her.

100 YEARS of PUBLISHING

Harold K. Guinzburg and George S. Oppenheimer founded Viking in 1925 with the intention of publishing books "with some claim to permanent importance rather than ephemeral popular interest." After merging with B. W. Huebsch, a small publisher with a distinguished catalog, Viking enjoyed almost fifty years of literary and commercial success before merging with Penguin Books in 1975.

Now an imprint of Penguin Random House, Viking specializes in bringing extraordinary works of fiction and nonfiction to a vast readership. In 2025, we celebrate one hundred years of excellence in publishing. Our centennial colophon will feature the original logo for Viking, created by the renowned American illustrator Rockwell Kent: a Viking ship that evokes enterprise, adventure, and exploration, ideas that inspired the imprint's name at its founding and continue to inspire us.

For more information on Viking's history, authors, and books, please visit penguin.com/viking.